AYN RAND

The Art of Fiction

A Guide for Writers and Readers

EDITED BY TORE BOECKMANN
INTRODUCTION BY LEONARD PEIKOFF

A PLUME BOOK

PLUME
Published by the Penguin Group
Penguin Putnam Inc., 375 Hudson Street, New York, New York 10014, U.S.A.
Penguin Books Ltd, 27 Wrights Lane, London W8 5TZ, England
Penguin Books Australia Ltd, Ringwood, Victoria, Australia
Penguin Books Canada Ltd, 10 Alcorn Avenue, Toronto, Ontario, Canada M4V 3B2
Penguin Books (N.Z.) Ltd, 182–190 Wairau Road, Auckland 10, New Zealand

Penguin Books Ltd, Registered Offices: Harmondsworth, Middlesex, England

First published by Plume, a member of Penguin Putnam Inc.

First Printing, January, 2000
10 9 8 7 6 5

Library of Congress Cataloging-in-Publication Data
Rand, Ayn.
The art of fiction: a guide for writers and readers / Ayn Rand; edited by Tore Boeckmann; introduction by Leonard Peikoff.
p. cm.
Includes index.
ISBN 0-452-28154-7
1. Fiction—Authorship. I. Boeckmann, Tore. II. Title.
PN3355 .R26 2000
808.3—dc21

99-35588
CIP

Printed in the United States of America
Set in Goudy

AYN RAND is the author of *Atlas Shrugged*, philosophically the most challenging bestseller of its time. Her first novel, *We the Living*, was published in 1936, followed by *Anthem*. With the publication of *The Fountainhead*, she achieved a spectacular and enduring success. Rand's unique philosophy, Objectivism, has gained a worldwide audience. The fundamentals of her philosophy are set forth in such books as *Introduction to Objectivist Epistemology*, *The Virtue of Selfishness*, *Capitalism: The Unknown Ideal*, and *The Romantic Manifesto*. *Journals of Ayn Rand* and *The Ayn Rand Reader* are available in Plume editions. Ayn Rand died in 1982.

LEONARD PEIKOFF is universally recognized as the world's premier Ayn Rand scholar. He worked closely with her for thirty years and was designated by Rand as the heir to her estate. He has taught philosophy at Hunter College, New York University, and the Polytechnic Institute of Brooklyn. Peikoff is the author of *The Ominous Parallels* and *Objectivism: The Philosophy of Ayn Rand*. For further information, go to his website: ALSHOW.com.

TORE BOECKMANN is an editor and publisher living in Norway. He has written on Ayn Rand's literary esthetics for *The Intellectual Activist*. His mystery fiction, originally published in *Alfred Hitchcock's Mystery Magazine*, has been anthologized in several languages.

CONTENTS

INTRODUCTION

This book is an edited version of an informal course of lectures given by Ayn Rand in her own living room in 1958. It was the year after the publication of *Atlas Shrugged*, and AR was at the peak of her powers as a novelist.

She gave the course, by "popular demand," to some twenty or so friends and acquaintances. She spoke extemporaneously, with only a few written notes naming the topics she meant to cover. Including questions and discussion, each of the twelve sessions lasted about four hours.

Two kinds of students attended: aspiring young fiction writers, and fiction readers from a variety of professions. These two groups are the audience to whom the present book is addressed.

The goal of the writers was obvious and practical: to learn everything possible about the problems and techniques of their craft. The readers, by contrast, of whom I was one, were there strictly as consumers; we wanted to enhance our enjoyment in reading. We wanted to know from the master what to look for in fiction and where it had come from, i.e., what had gone on behind the scenes, in the creator's mind, to produce the stories we loved (or hated). We were not content to grasp a book as a finished whole; we wanted to hear AR analyze the pleasures (or misery) a book evoked, and explain by what means its effects had been achieved.

Since AR held that fiction has four essential elements—theme, plot, characterization, and style—the lectures are organized accordingly, with the greatest emphasis on plot and style.

In regard to plot, AR identifies not only its nature and structure, but also its crucial relationships to theme and to a critical category of her own creation: "plot-theme." To concretize her theory, she analyzes many plots, some invented by her for the course, explaining what makes each good or bad and by what steps the bad ones could be methodically improved.

The tour de force of the book is its discussion of style, which occupies almost one half of the text. AR analyzes lengthy passages (describing love, nature, or New York City) from a variety of authors, often one sentence at a time. By juxtaposing different authors and by rewriting selected sentences, she identifies the essentials of several antithetical literary styles, showing in the process what different wordings do to a scene (and to a reader). Writers such as Victor Hugo, Sinclair Lewis, Thomas Wolfe, and Mickey Spillane are covered—as well as AR herself. By rewriting her own sentences, she shows in startling terms how seemingly minor, even trivial, changes can utterly destroy or reverse an artistic effect.

I can only hint here at other fascinating topics between these covers. AR explains how to stock one's own subconscious and thus create one's own "inspiration" as a writer. She explains what to do when one is blocked, or, in her words, suffering from "the squirms." She discusses drama versus melodrama; what makes a character intelligible and a characterization profound; the difference between authors who "tell" and those who "show"; the nature of proper versus sick or vicious humor; how to handle, or as reader evaluate, fantasy, tragedy, flashbacks, exposition, slang, metaphors; and much, much more.

AR was expert at philosophical detection. Although this course focuses on the principles of literature, it identifies—as AR characteristically does—the deepest philosophic issues involved. Those unfamiliar with philosophy will be astonished to discover the extent to which abstract issues—such as the mind-body question, or the free will-determinism controversy, or the advocacy of reason versus of faith—actually influence a writer of fiction, shaping his selection of events, his method of characterization, and even his way of combining words into a sentence.

AR's book on esthetics, *The Romantic Manifesto*, was based in part on the same 1958 lecture course. Because the *Manifesto* deals largely with art in general, however, there is little overlap with the present book. On the contrary, *The Art of Fiction* serves as an extended concretization of the Objectivist esthetics, and thus as an invaluable supplement to the *Manifesto*. Most of its content is unavailable in AR's other books.

Tore Boeckmann has done an outstanding job as editor. I suggested to him an extremely difficult assignment: to give us AR faithfully—the identical points and words—but freed of the awkwardness, the repetitions, the obscurities, and the grammatical lapses inherent in extemporaneous speech. Mr. Boeckmann has delivered superlatively. I have personally checked every sentence of the final manuscript. Now and then, I thought that some nuance within a sentence of AR's had been unnecessarily cut (these have been reinstated). Not once, however, did the editor omit, enlarge, or misrepresent AR's thought, not even in the subtlest of cases. Using the original lecture transcripts as his base, Mr. Boeckmann has produced the virtually impossible: AR's exact ideas and language—in the form of written expression, as against oral. This, I believe, is the only form in which AR herself would have wanted these lectures to be published.

If anyone wishes to check Mr. Boeckmann's accuracy, the original lectures are still available on cassette from Second Renaissance Books, 143 West Street, New Milford, CT 06776.

When I first read the manuscript, I was astonished to find how much, in the decades since 1958, I had forgotten. I had expected to move nostalgically through familiar material, but I found myself continually arrested by AR's unique insights and colorful illustrations. I was also moved by passages whose language and passion evoked for me the inimitable personality of AR herself.

You too can now experience the joys of attending a course in AR's living room. You cannot ask her questions, as I could. But you can soak up her answers.

If you do not know her philosophy of Objectivism, you will

probably be shocked by some of AR's ideas—but I am certain that you will not be bored. And I think that you will profit from the reading.

If you do share AR's philosophy, I know that you will enjoy this book.

—Leonard Peikoff
Irvine, California
September 1998

EDITOR'S PREFACE

Ayn Rand prepared for each of her lectures on fiction only by making some brief notes on a sheet or two of paper. For instance, the material presented here as Chapter 1 ("Writing and the Subconscious") was delivered on the basis of the following two sentences in her notes for the first lecture: "Is there an 'innate literary talent'? The relationship of the conscious and subconscious in fiction writing."

Given the extemporaneous nature of Ayn Rand's lectures, the transcript of the tape recordings had to be edited before publication. My editing was aimed at giving the material the economy, smoothness, and precision proper to written prose; it consisted primarily of cutting, reorganizing, and line editing.

In general, I cut discussions of issues that Ayn Rand later covered in *The Romantic Manifesto*. Most of my other cuts aimed at eliminating the repetitiveness typical of (and proper to) oral communication. Ayn Rand often stated a point several times, in slightly different words, to give her listeners time to absorb the point. In such cases, I selected the statement I judged superior, sometimes combining the best parts of different statements.

In the main, this book follows the structure of Ayn Rand's course. I did, however, make many minor transpositions within her general structure in order to conjoin related points or achieve a more logical progression of argument. Also, the book's chapter divisions follow the logic of the material rather than Ayn Rand's lecture breaks, since she often covered related material across those breaks. (The chapter and subchapter titles are mine.)

A lecture given by Ayn Rand in early 1959, as an addendum to her course, has been incorporated into this book (it forms the bulk of Chapter 4). Also included are some comments on fiction that she made in a 1969 course on *non*fiction writing. I am grateful to Robert Mayhew for bringing these to my attention. Finally, when Ayn Rand referred to passages in her own (or Sinclair Lewis's) novels, I sometimes supplied the relevant quote.

I made only a few editorial insertions. These are marked by square brackets, while parentheses always signal Ayn Rand's own asides.

The line editing consisted mainly of eliminating unnecessary words, rearranging the order of clauses within sentences, changing the tenses of verbs, etc. I also added words that were clearly implied by the original grammatical context (and necessary for a thought's completeness); and within that context, I made word changes where this improved the precision or economy of a sentence. I did not, however, freely restate any point in my own words. I am confident that none of my changes has altered Ayn Rand's intended meaning.

Nevertheless, the reader must bear in mind that the following pages have been edited by someone other than Ayn Rand herself. He must also remember the extemporaneous nature of the raw material.

In Chapter 8, Ayn Rand compares the conscientiously precise style of her own published works with the style of Victor Hugo, her favorite writer. Using a metaphor from painting, she says that "[Hugo's] brushstrokes are wider and more 'impressionistic' than [hers], whereas while [hers] are wide, someone who approached them with a microscope would see that every strand was put there for a purpose."

In this sense, the style of the present book may be described as more Hugoesque than Randian. The brushstrokes do represent Ayn Rand's views, but every strand does not necessarily reflect her purpose.

—Tore Boeckmann

1

Writing and the Subconscious

Suppose you start to write a story and your opening sentence describes a sunrise. To select the words of that sentence alone, you must have absorbed a great deal of knowledge which has become so automatic that your conscious mind need not pause on it.

Language is a tool which you had to learn; you did not know it at birth. When you first learned that a certain object is a table, the word *table* did not come to your mind automatically; you repeated it many times to get used to it. If you now attempt to learn a foreign language, the English word still leaps into your mind. It takes many repetitions before the foreign word occurs without your being conscious of groping for it.

Before you sit down to write, your language has to be so automatic that you are not conscious of groping for words or forming them into a sentence. Otherwise, you give yourself an impossible handicap.

In your description of a sunrise, you want to convey a certain mood; the sunrise, let us say, is an ominous one. That requires different words than a description of a bright, cheerful sunrise would. Consider how much knowledge goes into your ability to differentiate between the two intentions. What is ominous? What is cheerful? What kind of concepts, words, metaphors will convey each? All that was at one time conscious knowledge. Yet if you had consciously to select your words, including all the elements needed to establish a certain mood—if you had to go through the whole dictionary to decide which word to start with, and the same for the next word, and if you then had to go through all the possibilities of conveying the mood—your whole lifetime would not be enough to compose that one description.

What then do you do when you write a good description, fitting your purposes, within a reasonable amount of time according to your skill? You call on stored knowledge which has become automatic.

Your conscious mind is a very limited "screen of vision"; at any one moment, it can hold only so much. For instance, if you are now concentrating on my words, then you are not thinking about your values, family, or past experiences. Yet the knowledge of these is stored in your mind somewhere. That which you do not hold in your conscious mind at any one moment is your *subconscious*.

Why can a baby not understand this discussion? He does not have the necessary stored knowledge. The full understanding of any object of consciousness depends on what is already known and stored in the subconscious.

What is colloquially called "inspiration"—namely, that you write without full knowledge of why you write as you do, yet it comes out well—is actually the subconscious summing-up of the premises and intentions you have set yourself. All writers have to rely on inspiration. But you have to know where it comes from, why it happens, and how to make it happen to *you*.

All writers rely on their subconscious. But you have to know how to work with your own subconscious.

What you will find today is the exact opposite. Most writers cannot account even for why they chose to write a particular story, let alone for the manner in which they wrote it. In effect, they take the attitude of the worst medieval mystics. You have probably heard the mystic formula: "For those who understand, no explanation is necessary; for those who don't, none is possible." That is the slogan of religious mystics—and of artistic mystics. The simple meaning of that sentence is: "I don't know why I'm doing it, and I don't intend to explain."

If you do not want to be reduced to such a condition, you have to be conscious of your premises in general, and of your literary premises in particular. You have to train yourself to grasp your premises clearly, not merely as general rules with a few concretes to illustrate them, but with a sufficient number of concretes so that the full meaning of the premises becomes automatic to you. Every premise that you store in your subconscious in this manner—namely, thoroughly understood, thoroughly integrated to the concretes it represents—becomes part of your writing capital. When you then sit down to write, you do not need to calculate everything in a slow, conscious way. Your inspiration comes to the exact extent of the knowledge you have stored.

To describe a sunrise, you must have stored in your mind clear ideas of what you mean by "sunrise," what elements compose it, what kinds you have seen, what mood you want to project and why, and what kinds of words will project it. If you are clear on all these elements, they will come to you easily. If you are clear on some but not others, it will be harder to write. If you are not clear at all—if you have nothing but "floating abstractions" in your subconscious (by that I mean abstractions which you do not connect to concretes)—you will sit and stare at a blank sheet of paper. Nothing will come out of your mind because you have put nothing into it.

A writer, therefore, has to know how to use his subconscious, how to make his conscious mind use it as a Univac [an early computer]. A Univac is a calculating machine; but someone has to feed it the material and has to set the stops and make the selections if he wants a certain answer. You have to make your conscious mind do exactly that to your subconscious [computer]: you have to know what you are storing there and what kind of answers you are seeking. If you have stored the material properly, it will come to you.

Even so, there is no guarantee that you will work from nine to five at your desk and everything will always come out perfectly (unless you are a hack). What *is* guaranteed is that you will always be able to express exactly what you intended to express.

You have probably heard that no writer can ever fully express what he wanted to express; that every book is a disappointment to the author because it is only an approximation. Sinclair Lewis, a very good writer, once made such a remark. If you read his books, you will understand why. The themes that he wants to express are clear; the manner in which he expresses them is not always clear, particularly in the realm of emotions. He can express ideas and characterization up to a certain point, but in regard to deeper values, he is an unhappy repressor.

If a writer feels that he was unable fully to express what he wanted to express, it means that he did not know clearly what he wanted to express. He knew it only as a generalized package deal [a conglomeration of logically unrelated elements]; he had his theme defined approximately, but not sufficiently supported with full understanding of all the elements of that theme. That which you know clearly you can find the words for and you will express exactly.

If someone then challenges you and asks, "Why did you describe the sunrise in this way?" you will be able to answer. You will be able to give a conscious reason for every word in your description; but you did not have to know the reasons while writing.

I can give the reason for every word and every punctuation mark in *Atlas Shrugged*—and there are 645,000 words in it by the printer's count. I did not have to calculate it all consciously when I was writing. But what I did was follow a conscious intention in relation to the novel's theme and to every element involved in that theme. I was conscious of my purpose throughout the job—the general purpose of the novel and the particular purpose of every chapter, paragraph, and sentence.

To master the art of writing, you have to be conscious of why you are doing things—but do not edit yourself while writing. Just as you cannot change horses in the middle of a stream, so you cannot change premises in the middle of writing. When you write, you have to rely on your subconscious; you cannot doubt yourself and edit every sentence as it comes out. Write as it comes to you—then (next morning, preferably) turn editor and read over what you have written. If something does not satisfy you, ask yourself *then* why, and identify the premise you missed.

Trust your subconscious. If it does not deliver the kind of material you want, it will at least give you the evidence of what is wrong.

When you get stuck on a piece of writing, the reason is either that you have not sufficiently concretized the ideas you want to cover or that your purpose in this particular sequence is contradictory—that your conscious mind has given to your subconscious contradictory orders. I call this miserable state, which all writers know, "the squirms." It consists either of the inability to write anything or of the fact that your writing suddenly comes out badly—it does not flow as you want it to and does not express your intention.

Suppose you start to write a love scene. You write a few lines of dialogue, and suddenly you do not know what to say next. Let us say that it is a tragic love scene which has to end with the two characters renouncing each other. You know that they have to come to the parting, but not how to bring them there. Anything you put down is somehow not what you want; maybe the dialogue seems repetitious, or it is not too meaningful. So you try again, and whatever comes out is still not right. That's the squirms.

The trouble might lie in any one of the elements involved. It might be that you have not fully defined for yourself the attitude of the characters, or that you are not clear on the nature of the tragedy, or on the nature of love, or on the relationship of this particular scene to the rest of the novel. For each scene of a story, an enormously complex amount of material has to be held in mind; and, again, you cannot do it all consciously. You can hold only the highlights consciously, while relying on your subconscious to supply you with the missing connections and the concretes through which your general intention has to be expressed. If there is a contradiction in any one of those elements, it might stop you. And the difficult thing is that, in the nature of the process, you are stopped without having any clear idea of how to solve the problem.

The solution is always to think over every aspect of the scene and every connection to anything relevant in the rest of the book. Think until your mind almost goes to pieces; think until you are blank with exhaustion. Then, the next day, think again—until finally, one morning, you have the solution. Do enough thinking to give your subconscious ample time to integrate the elements involved. When those elements do integrate, the knowledge of what to do with the scene comes to you, and so do the words to express it. Why? Because you have cleared your subconscious files, your lightning calculator.

This experience is not confined to writers. With any kind of problem, you might think for days and suddenly, seemingly by accident, find the solution. The classic example is Newton and his apple: the apple fell on Newton's head and gave him the idea of the law of gravitation. As a writer once said: "Lucky accidents usually happen only to those who deserve them"*—meaning that Newton had worked for a long time on the problem which led him to the law of gravitation; the apple served merely as the last link integrating the conclusions he had already reached.

The same thing happens with a writer's inspiration or in breaking the squirms.

I have written many scenes which I did not plan in advance, beyond a general definition that "this scene will accomplish such and such a purpose"—yet when I came to them, they wrote themselves. Those scenes were usually the ones on which I was so clear—all the elements, intellectual, emotional, and artistic, were so familiar to me—that once I had set the general purpose, my subconscious did the rest. That is the happiest state a writer can reach and the most wonderful experience. You come to a scene and you feel as if somebody else is dictating it; you do not know what is coming, it is surprising you as it comes, you write almost in a blind trance—and afterward, when you reread it, it is almost perfect. You might need to change a few words, but the essence of the scene is there.

This is the kind of incident which gives rise to the idea that writing is an innate talent or that you write because some inner voice dictates to you. You have probably heard writers maintain that they are vehicles selected by a superior power because they hear this dictation. They will say: "I sit down to write a scene, I don't know what I'm going to write, and suddenly it comes to me. And it feels as if it's a voice dictating, so I'm sure it's the voice of God." In fact, it *does* feel that way. But what is the real meaning of this phenomenon?

This is a case of the accident that happens only to those who deserve it.

The writers who tell you that writing is an innate talent—that if you sit down to write, God either moves you or He does not, and if He

*Eliot Dole Hutchinson, *How to Think Creatively* (New York: Abingdon Press, 1949), p. 91.

does not, there is nothing you can do about it—these writers are not necessarily lying. They are merely poor introspectors. They do not know what enables *them* to write.

This type of writer usually writes himself out after a few years. As a rule, he starts rather young; he shows what is called "unusual promise"; and in a few years you see him repeating the same thing, less brilliantly and originally each time—and soon he finds that he has nothing to write about. That inspiration whose source he did not know has vanished. He does not know how to replenish it.

By imitation more than by understanding, he caught on to the process of writing; he grasped that people can put ideas, feelings, impressions down on paper, and he did so. If he has enough original observations stored in his subconscious, certain literary values might be present in his work for a while (among a lot of meaningless junk). But once he has used up that store of early impressions, he has nothing more to say. He merely grasped the general idea of what writing is, then coasted on his subconscious for a while, never attempting to analyze where his ideas came from, what he was doing, or why. Such a writer is antagonistic to any analysis; he is the type who tells you that "the cold hand of reason" is detrimental to his inspiration. He cannot function by means of reason, he says; if he begins to analyze, he feels, it will stop his inspiration altogether. (Given the way he functions, it *would* stop him.)

By contrast, if you know where your inspiration really comes from, you will never run out of material. A rational writer can stoke his subconscious just as one puts fuel in a machine. If you keep on storing things in your mind for your future writing and keep integrating your choice of theme to your general knowledge, allowing the scope of your writing to grow as your knowledge widens, then you will always have something to say, and you will find ever better ways to say it. You will not coast downhill after one outbreak of something valuable.

If part of your mind is still thinking, "Yes, but how do I know writing isn't an innate talent?" chances are that either you will not start writing at all, or you will start, but in perpetual terror. Each time you write something good, you will ask yourself: "But can I do it next time?"

I have heard many famous writers complain that they have literal anxiety attacks before starting a book. It does not matter how successful they are; since they do not fully know what the process of writing consists of—or, incidentally, why a book is or is not successful—they are always at the mercy of this terror: "Yes, ten novels were good, but how do I know that my eleventh one will be good?"

Instead of improving, these writers usually either maintain a precarious level or, more likely, deteriorate over the years. An example is Somerset Maugham. As far as one can gather his views from his writing, he does not believe that writing is a rational process; and his later works are much less interesting than his early ones. Though he has not quite written himself out, the quality has deteriorated.

In order to form your own literary taste and put it under your conscious control, always account for what you do or do not like in your reading—and always give yourself reasons. At first you might identify only the immediate reasons for your estimate of any given paragraph or book. As you practice, you will go deeper and deeper. (Do not memorize your premises. Merely store them in your subconscious; they will be there when you need them.)

It is possible for a writer to hold good literary premises by default, meaning: by imitation or by feeling. Many writers do, and thus cannot identify the reasons for their writing. They say, "I write because it just comes to me," and they fully believe that they have innate talent or that some mystical power dictates to them. Do not count on this mystical power to give *you* that talent. If you are tempted to ask, "Why can't *I* just rely on instinct?" my answer is that your "instinct" has not worked for you so far. You do not have writing premises; the mere doubt on your part is what indicates it. And even if you do have writing premises, or show what people conventionally call "indications of talent," you would stay on the same level for a whole career and never rise to writing what you really want.

To acquire literary premises, or to develop those you already have, what you need is *conscious* knowledge. That is what I offer in this course.

2

Literature as an Art Form

Literature is an art form which uses language as its tool—and language is an *objective* instrument.

You cannot seriously approach writing without the strict premise that words have objective meanings. If you approach it with the idea "I sort of know what I mean and my words sort of express something," you have only yourself to blame if people fail to grasp your intended meaning, or get the opposite meaning.

If you are not sure of a word, look it up in a dictionary (preferably an old dictionary, because the modern ones are nonobjective). But important words like *value*, *reason*, and *morality* are defined very loosely even in the better dictionaries. Do not use them in that loose manner; define specifically what you mean by those words, and make your meaning clear by the context in which you use them. This is an important rule of thinking for people generally, and an invaluable one for writers.

The writers who complain that they never express their meaning exactly are guilty among other faults of treating words as approximations, even in their own minds. Most writers today use words loosely; if you sort of get the drift of a paragraph, that is all you *can* get and all the writer intended. A famous example is Thomas Wolfe, who uses a vast number of words, none of them precisely. To see how not to write, read his descriptive passages. (I will discuss Wolfe in greater detail under Style.)

In regard to precision of language, I think I myself am the best writer today.

An exact writer treats words as he would in a legal document. This does not mean using awkward sentences. It means using words with absolute clarity, while still projecting violent emotion, color—any literary quality—by precise means.

A sentence in *Atlas Shrugged* that is applicable to all rational people, but particularly to writers, is the one where I say that Dagny "regarded language as a tool of honor, always to be used as if one were under oath—an oath of allegiance to reality." In regard to words, this should be the motto of every writer.

Since all art is communication, there can be nothing more viciously contradictory than the idea of nonobjective art. Anyone who wants to communicate with others has to rely on an objective reality and on objective language. The "nonobjective" is that which is dependent only on the individual subject, not on any standard of outside reality, and which is therefore incommunicable to others.

When a man announces that he is a nonobjective artist, he is saying that what he is presenting cannot be communicated. Why then does he present it, and why does he claim that it is art?

A nonobjective artist, whether a painter or a writer, is counting on the existence of objective art—and using it in order to destroy it.

Take a nonobjective painter. He creates some blobs of paint and proclaims that they are an expression of his subconscious, that they cannot be defined in any other terms, and that either you understand their meaning or you do not. Then he hangs them in a gallery. What does his work have in common with real art, which by definition represents recognizable physical objects? Only that it is hung on a wall. He has switched the definition of painting to "a piece of canvas in a frame."

The art world laughed at the first nonobjective paintings—and today such stuff is practically all that is produced. The result is the destruction of art as a meaningful activity. The field has been taken over by a self-appointed elite of mystics who are playing a game to delude those with money enough to buy their products. But their basic purpose is not material; it is to establish an unearned artistic aristocracy. (The same purpose was served by Toohey's clubs in *The Fountainhead.*) They want to make the practice of artistic creation available to anyone [regardless of ability], so that they can form their own little caste of specialists and pronounce, *subjectively*, what is and is not art. Then they can go around fooling each other and those who wish to support them.

In the field of literature, the nonobjective has not yet been accepted fully; but the elements of reason—and, therefore, of real art—are growing rarer and rarer in present-day writing. If the trend is not stopped, literature will follow the path of painting (and of all other aspects of our civilization).

The best-known example of a nonobjective writer is Gertrude Stein, who combines words into sentences without any grammatical structure or meaning. She is still to some extent laughed at, but people are laughing rather respectfully; their implied attitude is: "Well, she's strange, but her writing is probably deep." *Why* is it deep? "Because I, the reader, cannot understand it." (The subjectivism of the *audience* of nonobjective art is based on an inferiority complex which takes the form: "If I don't understand it, it must be profound.")

A writer who is *not* laughed at, but taught in universities as something very serious, is James Joyce. He is worse than Gertrude Stein; going all the way to the ultimate in nonobjective writing, he uses words from different languages, makes up some words of his own, and calls that literature.

When communication by means of language is discarded, what is left as the definition of writing? Writing becomes inarticulate sounds printed on paper by means of certain black marks.

No one can be consistently evil. Since evil is destruction, anyone who attempted consistently in his life to follow a bad premise would eliminate himself; he would be dead, or at best insane. A man can hold bad premises only so long as his good ones make them possible, support them—and are destroyed in the process of supporting them. Bad premises, if not eliminated, will grow and destroy the good ones.

I mention this for the following reason. If you are not fully committed to rationality and objectivity, you might not go as far as Stein and Joyce, but your writing will then be a *combination* of the rational and the irrational. You will not, say, write a book without any knowledge of its meaning; you know in general what you want to communicate, you stick to rationality in a loose way, and you write something that has the semblance of a story. But in selecting the details of that story—the characters, events, and sentences—you rely only on feelings and unidentified premises. These premises might be right or wrong; that which you do not know consciously is not in your control. If questioned, you say: "I know my general theme, but not why I wrote this particular sentence this way. I just felt like it."

This means that you will be a cross between a writer like me and a writer like Gertrude Stein.

Insofar as the rational elements predominate in your writing, you might "get away with" the flaws in your performance. But you should not want to be a part-rational, part-Gertrude Stein writer.

Do not let your own talent—your good premises—act in support of your bad premises and of the lazy or the irrational in your mind.

If to any extent you hold the premise of nonobjectivity, then by your own choice, you do not belong in literature, or in any human activity, or on this earth.

With the exception of proper names, every word is an abstraction. One way to have words come to you easily—words which express the exact shade of meaning you want—is to know clearly the concretes that belong under your abstractions.

For instance, the word *table* is an abstraction; it stands for any table you have ever seen or will see. If you try to project what you mean by "table," you can easily visualize any number of concrete examples. But in regard to abstractions like *individualism*, *freedom*, or *rationality*, most people are unable to name a single concrete. Even knowing one or two is not enough. In order to be completely free with words, you must know countless concretes under your abstractions.

The issue of the relationship of abstractions to concretes is crucial to all creative writing—not only to the composition of a sentence, but to the composition of a whole story and of its every chapter and paragraph.

When you compose a story, you start with an abstraction, then find the concretes which add up to that abstraction. For the reader, the process is reversed: he first perceives the concretes you present and then adds them up to the abstraction with which you started. I call this a "circle."

For instance, the theme of *Atlas Shrugged* is "the importance of reason"—a wide abstraction. To leave the reader with that message, I have to show what reason is, how it operates, and why it is important. The sequence on the construction of the John Galt Line is included for that purpose—to concretize the mind's role in human life. The rest of the novel illustrates the consequences of the mind's absence. In particular, the chapter on the tunnel catastrophe shows concretely what happens to a world where men do not dare to think or to take the responsibility of judgment. If, at the end of the novel, you are left with the impression "Yes, the mind is important and we should live by reason," these incidents are the cause. The concretes have summed up in your mind to the abstraction with which *I* started, and which I had to break down *into* concretes.

Every chapter and paragraph of *Atlas Shrugged* is set up on the same principle: What abstraction do I want to convey—and what concretes will convey it?

Young writers often make the following mistake: if they want a strong, independent, rational hero, they state in narrative that "he is strong, independent, and rational"—or they have other characters pay him these compliments in discussion. This does not convey anything. "Strong," "independent," and "rational" are abstractions. In order to leave your reader with those abstractions, you have to provide concretes that will make him conclude: "This man is strong, because he did X; independent, because he defied Y; rational, because he thought Z."

It is on your power to create this kind of circle that your success will rest.

The purpose of all art is the objectification of values. The fundamental motive of a writer—by the implication of the activity, whether he knows it consciously or not—is to objectify his values, his view of what is important in life. A man *reads* a novel for the same reason: to see a presentation of reality slanted according to a certain code of values (with which he may then agree or disagree).

(Do not be misled by the fact that many artists present depravity and ugliness: those are *their* values. If an artist thinks that life is depravity, he will do nothing but studies of sewers.)

To *objectify* values is to make them real by presenting them in concrete form. For instance, to say "I think courage is good" is not to objectify a value. To present a man who acts bravely, is.

Why is it important to objectify values?

Human values are *abstractions*. Before they can become real to or convince anyone, the concretes have to be given.

In this sense, every writer is a moral philosopher.

3

Theme and Plot

A novel's *theme* is the general abstraction in relation to which the events serve as the concretes.

For instance, the theme of *Gone With the Wind* is: the impact of the Civil War on the South—the destruction of the Southern way of life, which vanished with the wind. The theme of Sinclair Lewis's *Babbitt* is the characterization of an average American small businessman.

A novel's theme is not the same as its philosophical meaning. I could write (and would like to write) a detective story or a plain action thriller with no philosophical "message" and no long speeches—yet such a story would still implicitly convey all of my philosophy.

Fundamentally, what is important is not the message a writer projects *explicitly*, but the values and view of life he projects *implicitly*. Just as every man has a philosophy, whether he knows it consciously or not, so every story has an implicit philosophy. For instance, the theme of *Gone With the Wind* is historical, not philosophical—yet, if analyzed, the nature of the events and of the style would reveal the author's philosophy. By what he chooses to present, and by how he presents it, any author expresses his fundamental, metaphysical values—his view of man's relationship to reality and of what man can and should seek in life.

By contrast, a novel's *theme* need not be philosophical; it can be any general subject: a historical period, a human emotion, etc.

In judging a novel's esthetic value, all that one has to know is the author's theme and how well he has carried it out. Other things being equal, the wider a novel's theme, the better it is as a work of art. But whether one *agrees* with the theme or not is a separate question. If a novel presents a marvelous philosophical message but has no plot, miserable characterization, and a wooden style full of bromides, it is a bad work of art. On the other hand, I consider *Quo Vadis*, technically, one of the best-constructed novels ever written, yet I do not agree with its message: the rise and glorification of Christian culture.

On the subject of theme, I have one warning: *Be sure that your story can be summed up to some theme.*

In today's literature, many books do not have any abstract theme, which means that one cannot tell why they were written. An example is the kind of first novel that relates the writer's childhood impressions and early struggle with life. If asked why the particular events are included, the author says: "It happened to *me*." I warn you against writing such a novel. That something happened to *you* is of no importance to anyone, not even to you (and you are now hearing it from the archapostle of selfishness). The important thing about you is what you *choose* to make happen—your values and choices. That which happened by accident—what family you were born into, in what country, and where you went to school—is totally unimportant.

If an author has something of wider importance to say about them, it is valid for him to use his own experiences (preferably not too literally transcribed). But if he can give his readers no reason why they should read his book, except that the events happened to him, it is not a valid book, neither for the readers nor for himself.

Your theme, the abstract summation of your work, should be objectively valid, but otherwise the choice of themes is unlimited. You may write about deep-sea diving or anything you wish, provided you can show in the work why there is objective reason to be interested in it.

* * *

The most important element of a novel is *plot*. A plot is a purposeful progression of events. Such events must be logically connected, each being the outgrowth of the preceding and all leading up to a final climax.

I stress the word *events* because you can have a purposeful progression of ideas, or of conversations, without action. But a novel is a story about human beings in action. If you do not present your subject matter in terms of physical action, what you are writing is not a novel.

Let me give a few examples of the difference between theme and plot, starting with my own works.

The theme of *We the Living* is: the individual against the state, and, more specifically, the evil of statism. I present the theme by showing that the totalitarian state destroys the best people: in this case, a girl and the two men who love her. When I say that the story concerns a girl under a dictatorship and the men who love her, I am already talking about the plot.

Incidentally, if one names only the most general meaning of *We the Living*—the individual against the state—one does not indicate on whose side the author is. It could be a communist story showing the evil of the individual; but then the plot would be different. Or it could be a Naturalistic novel, a presentation of life under a dictatorship with no moral sides taken. The theme, however, would still be: the individual against the state. So when you work on a story of your own, make sure you define your theme clearly. That will help you judge what to include.

The theme of *The Fountainhead* is: individualism and collectivism, not in politics, but in man's soul. I show the effects of each principle on men's character by presenting the struggle of a creative architect against the society of his time.

To go from the theme to the plot line, you simply ask: By what means did the author present the theme? By this method, you can also identify a story's *plot-theme*, the essential line of its events. The plot-theme is the *focus* of the means of presenting the theme; for the writer, it is the most important element in creating a story. Your work as a novelist starts in earnest when you have chosen your story's plot-theme.

The theme of *Atlas Shrugged* is: the crucial value of the human mind. The plot-theme is: the mind on strike. The latter names an *action*—the central action to which all the other events of the story are related. It, therefore, is the plot-theme.

The theme of Victor Hugo's *Les Misérables* is: the injustice done to the lower classes of society. The plot-theme is: the struggle of an ex-convict to avoid the persecution of the police. This is the central narrative line, to which all the events are related.

The theme of *Gone With the Wind* is: the disappearance of the Southern way of life. The plot-theme is: the relationship of the heroine, Scarlett, to the two men in her life, Rhett Butler and Ashley Wilkes. These characters symbolize the historical forces involved. Scarlett is in love with Ashley, who represents the old South, but she can never win him; she is a Southern woman belonging in spirit with Rhett Butler, who represents the destruction of the old traditions and who pursues her throughout the story. This is an example of the skillful integration of plot to theme.

The theme of Sinclair Lewis's *Main Street* is the presentation of a typical American small town. The plot-theme is the struggle of a girl of more intellectual trends to bring culture to this town—her struggle with the materialistic small-town attitude of everybody around her. I must stress, however, that *Main Street* (like all of Lewis's novels) does not have a plot in the sense of a *structure* of events.

The main distinction between a Romantic and a Naturalistic novel is that a Romantic novel has a plot whereas a Naturalistic novel is plotless. But although it does not have a *purposeful* progression of events, a good Naturalistic novel still has a series of events which add up to a story. In such a case, when I say "plot-theme," I mean the central line of those events.

Take Tolstoy's *Anna Karenina*, the novel most typical of the Naturalistic school. It is the story of a married woman who falls in love with another man, leaves her husband, and finds herself hopelessly doomed. Since she is ostracized by society, she has no friends and nothing to do with her time, and eventually she and her lover grow bored with each other. The man, an officer by profession, volunteers for an army assignment in some Balkan war. The implication is that he will be killed; but he wants to go because he cannot stand his solitary confinement with the woman he loves. She commits suicide by jumping under the wheels of a train (in a horribly well-written scene).

The woman is presented as a sympathetic character; her outstanding quality is her eagerness to live. The husband is deliberately presented as a conventional mediocrity without any values or distinction; all the evidence is given as to why the woman's life with him is boring and meaningless. Yet she dares to break the conventions because she wants to be happy—which the author considers an insufficient reason. There is no life for anyone outside of society, he implies; so, right or wrong, one has to accept social standards. The abstract theme is: the evil of adultery and, more broadly, of the pursuit of happiness. The plot-theme is: A woman leaves her husband and is destroyed for her unconventionality.

The basic philosophical premises which determine whether a writer belongs to the Naturalistic or the Romantic school are the premises of determinism or of free will. If a writer's basic conviction is that man is a determined creature—that he has no choice, but is the plaything of fate or his background or God or his glands—that writer will be a Naturalist. The Naturalistic school, in essence, presents man as helpless; it has some great writers, but it is an evil school philosophically, and its *literary* flaw is plotlessness. A plot, being a purposeful progression of events, necessarily presupposes men's freedom to choose and their ability to achieve a purpose. If a writer believes that men are determined beings, he will not be able to devise a plot.

(A writer is governed by his deepest conviction, rather than by some professed belief. He might claim to be a believer in free will but subconsciously be a determinist, or vice versa. His subconscious premise is what will show in the structure of his writing.)

The Romantic school of literature approaches life on the premise that man has free will, the capacity of choice. The distinguishing mark of *this* school is a good plot structure.

If man has the capacity of choice, then he can *plan* the events of his life; he can set himself purposes and achieve them. If so, his life is not a series of accidents. Events do not "just happen" to him; he *chooses* what he makes happen (and if accidents occur, his purpose is to overcome them). He is the architect of his own life.

If such is your view of man, you will write about events dealing with a man's purposes and the steps by which he achieves them. That is what constitutes a plot. A plot is "a purposeful progression of events"—not an accidental string of occurrences, but a progression centered on someone's purpose (usually the hero's or heroine's).

Here I call your attention to Aristotle's concepts of *efficient* and *final* causation.

Efficient causation means that an event is determined by an antecedent cause. For instance, if you strike a match to a gasoline tank and it explodes, the striking of the match is the cause and the explosion is the effect. This is what we normally mean by causality as it exists in physical nature.

Final causation means that the end result of a certain chain of causes determines those causes. Aristotle gave this example: A tree is the final cause of the seed from which that tree will grow. From one perspective, the seed is the *efficient* cause of the tree: first there is the seed, and as a result, the tree grows. But from the perspective of *final* causation, Aristotle said, the future tree determines the nature of the seed and of the development it has to follow in order to end up as that tree.

This, by the way, is one of my major differences from Aristotle. It is wrong to assume what in philosophy is known as *teleology*—namely, that a purpose set in advance in nature determines physical phenomena. The concept of the future tree determining the nature of the seed is impossible; it is the kind of concept that leads to mysticism and religion. Most religions have a teleological explanation of the universe: God made the universe, so His purpose determined the nature of the entities in it.

But the concept of final causation, properly delimited, *is* valid. Final causation applies only to the work of a conscious entity—specifically of a *rational* one—because only a thinking consciousness can choose a purpose ahead of its existence and then select the means to achieve it.

In the realm of human action, everything has to be directed by final causation. If men allow themselves to be moved by efficient causation—if they act like determined beings, propelled by some immediate cause outside themselves—that is totally improper. (Even then, volition is involved: if a man decides to abandon purpose, that is also a choice, and a bad one.) Proper human action is action by means of *final* causation.

An obvious example here pertains to writing. As a writer, you must follow the process of final causation: you decide on the theme of your book (your purpose), then select the events and the sentences that will concretize your theme. The reader, by contrast, follows the process of *efficient* causation: he goes step by step through your book being moved toward the abstraction you intended.

Any purposeful activity follows the same progression. To make an automobile, a man first has to decide what kind of object he is making—an automobile—and then select the elements which, put together, will constitute that automobile. By the process of final causation, he makes nature perform the necessary processes of efficient causation; he puts together certain parts in a certain scientific order to achieve a vehicle which moves.

In nature, there is no final causation; but in *man's* action, final causation is the only proper guide.

Observe how this applies to the issue of plot stories versus plotless ones. In a plot story, men and events are pulled forward by a purpose. In a Naturalistic, plotless story, they are pushed from behind, as in physical nature.

Take the novels of Sinclair Lewis again. They are not totally formless: they begin somewhere and end somewhere. But the characters rarely pursue any particular goals. They go through certain events, drawing some conclusions, growing or deteriorating mentally, in a haphazard interaction between themselves and their social background. Their actions do proceed from their characters *as the author sees them*, but the protagonists do not determine the course of their lives.

There is a fundamental contradiction in the premise of the Naturalistic school. You are interested in reading a Naturalistic story such as *Anna Karenina* only because of the implied assumption that the characters have choice. If a woman hesitates between leaving her husband for the man she loves and giving up the man she loves for her husband, this is a crucial choice in her life. It can interest you only if you assume she *has* choice about it and you want to know why she decides the way she does and whether she is right or wrong. If, however, you hold firmly in mind the idea that she cannot choose but has to do whatever fate determines—and that, should you ever be in a comparable situation, your future action is unknowable to you because something other than your choice will determine *your* decision—the story will have no meaning for you whatever.

If men have no choice, you cannot write a story about them, nor is there any sense in reading one. If they *do* have choice, there is no sense in reading about unchosen events. What you rationally want to read is a story about men's choices, right or wrong—about their decisions and what they *should* have decided—which means: a free-will, Romantic plot story.

Now let us consider in more detail the issue of plot.

If a man is not a determined being but sets his own purpose, then it is *he* who has to achieve that purpose and devise the means to achieve it. This means that some *action* is necessary on his part. If his action meets with no obstacles—if a man decides to go to the corner grocery, and he goes, buys his groceries, and comes home—this is a purposeful action, but not a story. Why not? Because there was no *struggle* involved.

To illustrate the achievement of a purpose, you have to show men overcoming obstacles. This statement pertains strictly to writers. Metaphysically—in reality—one does not need obstacles in order to achieve a purpose. But you as a writer need to *dramatize* purpose, i.e., you have to isolate the particular meaning that you want your events to illustrate—by presenting it in a *stressed* action form.

For instance, in *The Fountainhead* I show the career of a creative, independent architect. It is possible (although not probable) that in real life he would immediately find the right clients and achieve great success without any opposition. But that would be completely wrong artistically. Since my purpose is to show that a man of creative independence will achieve his goal regardless of any opposition, a story in which there *is* no opposition would not dramatize my message. I have to show the hero in a difficult struggle—and the worse I can make it, the better dramatically. I have to devise the hardest obstacles possible, and those of greatest significance to the hero.

For instance, if the hero has a distant cousin who disapproves of his career, that is not a great obstacle to overcome. But if the woman he loves objects to his career and tempts him to give it up, and he says, "No, I prefer to be an architect," and thus risks losing her forever, that is real dramatization. Then the hero is in the middle of a clash of two values and has to choose the right one (which he does).

The more struggle a story involves, the better the plot. By showing the kind of conflicts that a man has to resolve and make the right decision about, the author shows which decision *is* right, or, in the case of characters who make the wrong decision, why the decision is wrong, to what bad consequences it leads.

The essence of plot structure is: struggle—therefore, conflict—therefore, climax. A struggle implies two opposing forces in conflict, and it implies a climax. The climax is the central point of the story, where the conflict is resolved.

"Conflict" here means conflict with other men or conflict within a man, but not conflict against nature or coincidence.

For the purpose of dramatizing a man's struggle and choice, a conflict within his own mind, which is then expressed and resolved in action, is one of the best devices. By that means, you present clearly and in action the man's freedom—the fact that *his* decision is what resolves the conflict.

A man's struggle against nature, by contrast, is an issue of free will only on his part, not on the part of nature. The blind forces of nature can be only what they are and do only what they do. A conflict against nature is therefore not a dramatic conflict—no choice or suspense is possible on the part of the inanimate adversary. In a fully volitional conflict, both adversaries must have free will; two choices, two sets of values, must be involved.

Coincidence is always bad in writing, and it is disastrous in plot writing. Only lesser plot writers, usually bad mystery novelists, characteristically employ coincidence, though some great writers, like Hugo, are guilty of it at times. But it is to be avoided at all costs. A plot presents free will and a man's achievement of, or at least struggle for, his purpose—and coincidence is irrelevant to anyone's choice or purpose. It can happen in life, but it is meaningless. So do not write the kind of stories in which a conflict is suddenly resolved by a natural disaster, such as a flood or an earthquake that conveniently kills the villain at the right moment.

A plot, as I have said, is "a purposeful progression of events." The word *purposeful* here has two meanings: not only must the *characters* be purposeful, but also, in order to have an integrated story, the *author* must be purposeful. The events of a plot story are always connected to the main goals of the characters *and* to a growing conflict which *directs* the events (and which has to be resolved in some decisive manner at the end).

Take *Les Misérables*. The hero steals a loaf of bread and is sent to prison. He cannot stand it, so he tries to escape; he draws a longer sentence. When he is finally released, he is an outcast. He comes to a town where nobody will lodge him or serve him dinner. Then he sees a house with an open door—the house of the local bishop. This very well-drawn, altruistic bishop invites him to stay, serves him a meal, and treats him with all the deference due an honored guest. The ex-convict notices the bishop's only valuable possessions: real silverware and two silver candelabra on the mantelpiece. In the middle of the night, the trusted ex-convict steals the silverware and escapes.

Given the man's enormously embittered state, the reader can understand why he makes this choice. It is an evil choice, but it proceeds from the previous events of the story.

Then he is caught and brought back to the bishop by local policemen who recognize the silverware. They tell the bishop: "We've caught this ex-convict and he says that you gave him the silverware." And the bishop says: "Yes, of course I gave it to him. But, my friend, why did you forget to take the candelabra, which I also gave you?" The police depart, and the bishop tells the ex-convict: "Take this silver. With it I am buying your soul from the devil and giving it to God."

That is a scene. It is a beautifully dramatic example of turning the other cheek.

The bishop believes that his action will have a good effect; and the hero does reform, though not immediately. But everything he does is always conditioned by what he concluded (or misconcluded) from a previous event; and the actions of the police thereafter are always conditioned by their suspicion of him. The events are determined by the goals that the characters want to accomplish, *and* each event is necessitated by the preceding one—necessitated not deterministically, but *logically*. "If A, then B logically had to follow."

By contrast, the events of a Naturalistic novel do not proceed one from the other, but are largely haphazard. A Naturalist has no principle by which to decide whether to show a family picnic, a day of shopping, a flower show, or a breakfast. The events are intended to present or influence the characters—and *that* is the author's standard of selection. The central line is always the development of a given character; and the author stops when he thinks that he has presented the character well enough for the reader to understand him.

The predominance of characterization over action is the Naturalist's distinguishing premise. Something does happen, but *what* happens is of less importance than what it reveals about the characters. For instance, Babbitt [a real estate agent] sells a new house, and the reader learns a great deal about his psychology. The event is not much; the meaning is in the characterization.

An event is an action taken in reality. If a character goes to the grocery store, this is an event, but not a very meaningful one—it is a random, Naturalistic event. If a character meets a man on the street and shoots him, this is a *potentially* meaningful event, if you discover its motivation. If the character took the action because of a previous event which forced him to make a choice, then the action is a plot event.

Closely allied with the issue of plot, as an attribute of it, is the issue of *suspense*.

If you cannot put down a novel, or if you sit on the edge of your theater seat, that is your emotional reaction to the fact that the story has suspense. Try to recall any story that held you in this manner. You will find that the story is one in which the author *lets you in on his purpose*.

In a suspenseful story, the events are constructed in such a manner that the reader has reason to wonder about the outcome. If an author tells you what is going to happen, the story will not hold your interest. But neither will you be interested if you do not know at all where the story is going—if it is a jumble of arbitrary events, or even if it has an inner logic which you discover later, but the author never showed you what to expect.

The archetype of a suspense scene is the one in *Atlas Shrugged* where Rearden enters Dagny's apartment and meets Francisco. Why *must* this scene hold the reader's interest? Because he has long been given grounds to wonder what will happen to all three when the two men discover each other's relationship to Dagny. I have let him in on what to expect. I have planted that Rearden is anxious to discover the name of Dagny's past lover, and that Francisco still loves her and hopes she has waited for him. The reader therefore knows that when these three find out the truth, some strong reactions will occur, the nature of which he cannot predict for certain. This is what makes him read the scene with interest.

Suppose, however, that Rearden knew everything about Dagny's past, and Francisco suspected that Dagny would fall for Rearden; then, the day after the beginning of the Dagny-Rearden romance, Francisco comes to visit her and learns the truth. Would this be interesting or suspenseful? No. Since the reader has been given no reason to attach any importance to the characters' learning the truth, there is no conflict, no drama, nothing to wonder about.

If you want to hold your readers, give them something to wonder about. I once knew a Hollywood scenario writer who had a graphic expression of her own for this point. When she started work on a story, she said, she always established a "worry line"—a line of problems for the audience to worry about.

To do that, you have to know not only how to build your suspense—how to feed the reader information step by step—but also how to establish the kind of conflict that in reason will interest a reader. Suppose Dagny dyed her hair blond and worried how her brother James would react. If they were the kind of characters who could worry about such an issue, neither they nor the issue would be interesting. When you set up a line of suspense, ask yourself: Is there any reason why anyone should be interested in this conflict? Are these values important enough to worry about?

To illustrate why plot is important and how it relates to a story's theme and suspense, I want to project what would happen to some of the issues in *Atlas Shrugged* and *The Fountainhead* if they were treated plotlessly.

For instance, the meaning of the Dagny-Rearden romance in *Atlas*

Shrugged is that their shared ideas, values, and struggle is the root of their love. Consider what a non-plot writer would have done with this material. Dagny would come to Rearden's office, they would start talking, and suddenly he would draw her into his arms and they would kiss. This is realistic, it can happen—but it does not have much dramatic value. The same scene could have happened between any two people, including villains such as James Taggart and Betty Pope.

By contrast, in *Atlas Shrugged* I bring about Dagny and Rearden's love scene at the height of their mutual triumph, in connection with the achievement which unites their careers: the opening of the John Galt Line. I make them admit their love during an event which presents *in action* the ideas and values they have in common. This is an example of presenting an issue in plot terms.

Or take the quarry scene in *The Fountainhead*, where Dominique meets Roark. She is an extreme hero-worshiper; she has declared that she will never fall in love except with someone great; and she does not want to find a great man because she thinks he would be doomed. If, while researching one of her newspaper columns, she had met Roark as a rising architect, that would not have been dramatic. But it *is* dramatic for her to meet the ideal man at the bottom, as nothing but a quarry worker. She had feared that the world would crush a hero—and the scene brings her face-to-face with the fact that no matter what the world does to him, a hero *is* a value, and one she cannot resist.

Now take the scene in *Atlas Shrugged* where Rearden quits. Throughout the story, a man's going on strike had involved two elements: the victim's realization that he *is* and should stop being a victim, and his conviction that he cannot continue his work under the present setup. Therefore, when I have Rearden quit, two elements are necessary: Rearden's final realization that he *should* go on strike, and the final atrocity of the looters which makes him decide that the situation is hopeless. The demand that he work at a loss in order to support his worst enemies, plus the government-engineered assault on his mills, dramatizes the whole issue of the strike, specifically as it applies to Rearden's life.

Consider how a non-plot writer would make Rearden go on strike. Rearden would be sitting at his desk or walking down a country road, thinking the situation over, and he would decide: "Things are pretty bad. I can't stand it any longer. I'll quit." A decision like this might be perfectly proper in real life, but it makes for a lousy story. Such a decision is a purely psychological development, without any action to show the nature and elements of the decision.

Take Dagny, the last of the strikers. So long as she does not understand the death premise in the villains, she thinks, justifiably, that they will ultimately recognize that she is right. Only when she understands the truth—when, at the banquet, she sees the attitude of James Taggart and his crowd toward John Galt and learns that they are going to torture him—is she ready to quit.

If nothing else had happened, however, this would have been a somewhat unsatisfactory way of making her go on strike. That which had represented her tie to the world—her railroad—would not have been directly involved. To dramatize properly Dagny's act of going on strike, I had to place her in a situation where she must choose between the strike and her railroad. This was the right moment, therefore, to bring in the issue of the collapsing bridge. Dagny leaps to the telephone, hesitates for a last moment—and then the strike wins.

This moment has emotional appeal because it unites all the issues of Dagny's life—and does so not merely in her mind, but *in action*. An event takes place, and she has to make a decision about it.

Think of other Romantic plot novels you have read and name to yourself the meaning of the events. Then project what would happen if the same issues were presented without action—i.e., if the conflicts were resolved merely in someone's mind, while the outward event was nothing but someone sitting in a room or walking down the street. The result would be plotlessness.

To write a plot story, you have to be clear on what issues you want to present and then think of the events that will present those issues *in action*. In all the above illustrations, I had to find that which is essential to the issue and then build an event around it.

If Rearden decides to quit while sitting at his desk, the fact that he is sitting at his desk is irrelevant to the issue being resolved. Suppose he is driving his automobile and has a traffic accident which makes him interrupt his thinking long enough to call a garage. He is involved in *some* action while making his decision about quitting, but the action is totally irrelevant to the decision. Or suppose nothing happens on the day Rearden quits, except that Wesley Mouch telephones him from Washington and is rude; i.e., the last straw is a bureaucrat's bad manners. This has *something* to do with the issue of rebelling against the looters, but it is not *essential* to that issue.

Train your mind to think in essentials, not on issues of literature only, but on *all* issues. This is important for writing a good plot story, and it is even more important for your own life. You do not want a life which is a badly constructed story—a series of unrelated episodes with no purpose, progression, or climax.

You can have a good life structure, as well as a good plot structure, by one method only: you must know essentials. You must recognize what is the *important* thing in any issue you deal with.

4

The Plot-Theme

The plot-theme is the central conflict that determines the events of a plot. It is the seed enabling you to develop a whole plot structure.

I have said that both the author and the characters of a novel have to be purposeful. In discussing the issue of plot-theme, I am concerned with the *first* of these points—with how an *author* sets himself a plot purpose.

Also, I talk here only about plot, not about theme—about you as dramatist, not you as philosopher. If you have a message, that message determines your plot-theme; if not, you start with the plot-theme. In either case, however, the proper literary work starts when you begin to construct a plot—and on this part of the job, *the plot comes above your message*. I do not mean that you can ever decide on a plot which contradicts your message—if it does, you must select a different plot. I mean only that the plot must be your sole consideration *while you are constructing it*.

Therefore, when I talk here about the author's purpose, I mean the plot purpose.

First I will discuss the nature of conflict.

Anything that a man desires and acts to achieve is a value, at least to him. (Whether the value is rational is a different question.) Therefore, a "conflict of values" does not necessarily mean some vast philosophical abstraction. Do not think that it means at least "communism versus capitalism," and that nothing less will do.

If you look at a menu in a restaurant and have to decide whether to order ice cream or cake for dessert, that is a conflict of values. If you do not like cake, only ice cream, there is no conflict. But if you like both and are unable to eat both, you must decide which to choose—and there is a momentary conflict until you do.

This is not the kind of conflict on which you can build a story. Since the values involved in a story should be important enough to interest the characters, the author, and the reader, a conflict over a choice of dessert obviously will not do. But the point is that, even in such a small issue, there *is* a clash of values.

Now observe that stories about criminals usually form good plot structures. Crime stories are the most primitive, and most common, form of suspense dramas. (Today, unfortunately, we have nothing *but* crime stories if we want to read a plot story.)

The reason is that a criminal by definition has a conflict of values. He wants, let us say, to rob a bank for the loot. At the same time, he does not want to be arrested. He wants *both* his safety and the product of an action which endangers his safety. Therefore, the moment you introduce a crime into a story, you have a rudimentary, but proper, conflict of serious values.

Project a story in which the lead character is a bank robber who does not care whether he is arrested. He has decided that he will have security in jail, so he does not attempt to hide or escape. The story would be totally static. Or let us say that he robs a bank in a city where there are no policemen, so that nobody intends to do anything about it. No plot would be possible.

To appreciate what makes a good plot situation, you must identify not only a character's *specific* purpose, but also all the conflicts that this purpose necessarily engenders. If you say of a criminal, "His purpose is to rob," that is not yet a conflict. You must remember that his purpose is also to escape.

Consider my short story "Good Copy" [see *The Early Ayn Rand*]. Laury, the main character, is a small-town reporter. He wants to stir up excitement in order to further his career, so he stages a kidnapping. By doing so, he risks arrest, disgrace, and the *loss* of his career. This is already a simple conflict.

Next, he falls in love with the girl whom he has kidnapped, and she falls in love with him. This introduces a new clash of values. Laury has done something evil to the girl he loves (or at least he himself would identify it as evil). And the girl has fallen in love with her own kidnapper, which is not the same as falling in love with a man whom she immediately recognizes as a real hero. If a girl falls in love with an apparent criminal and then discovers that in fact he justifies her love, that is a happily *resolved* conflict, but still a conflict.

Next, when a real criminal enters the scene and steals the girl from Laury, Laury is placed in his top conflict; to save the girl, he must surrender to the police, go to jail, and perhaps ruin his career. His career is now in conflict with his love.

That is a plot-theme.

Consider what would happen to this story if some of its elements were omitted. Suppose Laury kidnapped an adult man—say, a nasty villain. The conflict would be much simpler and less serious. Since Laury does not care about his prisoner, he is in an easier position from the start; and if a real criminal then steals the prisoner from him, he might or might not decide to go to the police. Perhaps he might send in an anonymous tip, but not risk his own arrest. Not too much is at stake.

Or suppose Laury is not a reporter, but a real criminal, and he falls in love with a girl he has kidnapped. It would not then endanger his *career* if he confesses and is arrested. There is no great clash of values.

When you look for a plot-theme, you must look for a central conflict—and not merely a one-line conflict, but a conflict complex enough to make constructing a story possible.

Suppose you name as your initial plot assignment: A young man fakes a crime to stir up a dead town. That is an action, but not a conflict. There is no clash of values, neither within the man himself nor between him and others. Maybe the dead town is eager to be stirred up.

Or suppose you start with the idea: A young man fakes a crime, which turns into a real crime when a real criminal interferes. That is not much of a conflict, and not much of a story can be built around it. The young man is put in an uncomfortable position, but one he can correct easily. To make possible a progression of events, some other element has to be added, such as the man's falling in love with the victim of his crime. Then you have a real conflict with many facets.

The best way to see what kind of conflict can serve as a plot-theme is from the inside. So let us start a story from scratch.

Suppose you decide to start and you face a blank. You cannot start from nowhere; you must start with something. So you decide, say, on a background: the Middle Ages.

Again you face a blank, because from here on you can do anything; you can write about any aspect of the Middle Ages. And if something can be anything, it is actually nothing; if you feel, "Now I can write anything," you will write nothing. Only when you have some specific entity in mind—some germ of a plot—can you make something out of something and begin to build.

Since plot is essentially conflict, you must look for a good conflict. So you decide that since the Middle Ages was a religious period, the best figure for your story is, say, a priest. If this priest merely practices his religion, you have no story. You must put him in a conflict. If he is a medieval priest who takes his religion seriously, the best possible conflict would be a sexual passion—because that is what his religion forbids him. If his values all pertain to another dimension, the worst thing for him would be to acquire a strong value pertaining to this earth—to fall in love.

The next question is: with whom? If he falls in love with a young nun who shares his values, that might be dramatic. But it is much more dramatic if he falls in love with someone who represents the opposite of his values—with a symbol of this earth: a Gypsy dancer.

The next question is: does she love *him*? If she does, he might be in conflict with his conscience and with society, but at least his love is rewarded. However, if he is tempted to betray his religion for the sake of a guilty passion, it is a more tragic and therefore stronger conflict if the girl does *not* love him.

The next question is: does she love anyone else? Obviously, it is worse for him if she does.

The next question is: if he attempts to pursue her, will anyone defend her? Yes, there is more conflict if someone will. Who? If the girl's defender is a stranger to the priest, he poses a mere factual obstruction. But what if her defender is a protégé whom the priest brought up out of charity—the symbol to the priest of his own religious duty properly performed?

Now consider the conflicts of the other characters. The protégé is in a terrible conflict between his love for the girl and his devotion to his benefactor. The girl, being pursued by the priest (who in the Middle Ages would be very powerful), is torn between her love for the other man and a threat to her life.

This is the plot-theme of *Notre-Dame de Paris*.

I am certain that Victor Hugo did not need this kind of logical analysis. The inexhaustible ingenuity for plot shown in his plays indicates that writing and conflict were nearly synonymous to him. He had such a grasp of the nature of conflict that its projection became automatic.

When a man grasps the nature of conflict, he knows what is dramatic. To him, it may feel as if a plot idea is inspirational: "I just thought of it." But you have to get to the stage where you have earned this kind of inspiration.

When you compose a story, your mind does not go through the steps I outlined. If you know a plot in advance, you can easily ask the right questions; but when you start from scratch, so many possibilities exist at each turn that you cannot go through them consciously. You have to let your subconscious be the selector—and it can become the selector, throwing you the right, most dramatic situations, only if you know what conflict is and why it is necessary. When you know this, and when you have practiced by laboriously composing a few plots, your imagination begins to work automatically and saves you a lot of the steps.

What I have so far described of *Notre-Dame de Paris* is not the plot, but the plot-theme. The writer's job is not finished. But once you have this kind of central conflict, you do not have an "anything" anymore. You have set a limit to the nature of your story, a limit that will be your standard of selection in regard to events.

If you are not clear on your plot-theme, your story will fall apart; it will have no logical continuity. Also, you yourself will not know what to do. You will start to include events because you feel like it, probably on the principle of association. One scene makes you feel something else, so you write another which has nothing to do with your central line. Your story is going nowhere, and you do not know where to go.

Before you construct a story, you must decide on the central conflict, which will then serve as the standard telling you what you have to include in order to fully develop this conflict, and what is superfluous.

Let me give a few more examples of plot-themes.

Suppose you want to write a love story. If two persons are in love, that is not a conflict; you have to make their love clash with some serious value of theirs. Suppose they belong to opposite nations at war. A plot is now *possible*, but not if they merely sit at home and long for each other; what you need is to put them into an *action* conflict. Let us say he is an army officer and she a spy for the other side, with a dangerous secret to reveal, and you bring them to a position where he has to either let her escape or shoot her to save his country. This is the kind of conflict that can serve as a plot-theme—it has enough material in it to give you the line for a story (an unoriginal one, but bromides, it is said, became bromides because they were good the first time).

Suppose you want to write a story about unrequited love. If a man is desperately in love with a woman, but she is not in love with him, that is not yet a conflict. But suppose she has to marry him for some outside reason—to get an inheritance, or to be allowed to stay in America—and he agrees to marry her in name only. Conflict, and thus the possibility of a good story, is immediately introduced.

Plot conflict is not conflict merely in a character's mind or soul, while he sits at home. A plot conflict has to be *expressed in action*. When you construct a plot, therefore, you must be a "materialist" and concern yourself only with values and issues that *can* be expressed in physical action.

Not everything is dramatizable by means of plot. For instance, the theme of *Anthem* is the word *I*, and the story is built around one idea: What would happen if a man lost the concept *I*, and how would he regain it? This is not a plot-theme, because it is internal.

In *Anthem*, there is no plot—no conflict of two or more persons against each other. The hero's adversary is the collective as such; and the collective has no particular purpose beyond objecting to him escaping. He is not fighting individuals, but the whole system. By contrast, *We the Living*, my most tightly plotted story, has not only a social message, the evil of a collectivist society, but also a conflict among specific persons. The story is not "Kira [the heroine] against the state"; the villain is actually Andrei, along with such lesser representatives of the communist system as Syerov, Sonia, and Victor. Had it been "Kira against the state," the story would have been plotless.

Anthem is a psychological fantasy, not a full-scale indictment of collectivism. The collective is brought in only to explain why the hero is in the predicament of not having the concept *I*. Had I introduced a plot, I would have taken the story away from the main subject, because the issue of what happens in your mind when you lack a certain concept is not an action theme.

In my short story "The Simplest Thing in the World" [see *The Romantic Manifesto*], the hero sits at a desk, struggles to write something, and decides that he cannot. The story takes place in his mind; it is strictly an illustration of the psychological process of creation. It is as plotless as anything could be.

Let us examine a few more plot-themes.

The oldest and tritest is that of the prostitute with a heart of gold. Why is it so popular? Because a prostitute has cut herself off from all human values. Her profession clashes with any other value she might want—respectability, a career, anything—and the worst clash comes if she falls in love. Then a dramatic story is an immediate possibility.

Usually, the prostitute falls in love, decides to abandon her profession, and then struggles not to let the man find out the truth about her past. This is the pattern of *Anna Christie*, *Anna Lucasta*, and many lesser-known stories. The conflict is resolved in one of two ways: the man always finds out the truth, and then he either accepts it and forgives her (a happy ending), or he denounces her and commits suicide, and she jumps out of a window (a tragic ending). This is all that most people have done with this particular conflict.

To see how the conflict can be improved, ask yourself how one can make it harder for the heroine. Suppose her lover knows of her past and has forgiven it, but then she discovers that if he marries her, he will ruin his career. He will never be able to succeed at what *he* wants if his wife is a former prostitute. He will not give her up, so she has to *make* him give her up, which she can do only by pretending that she is *still* a prostitute. She has to hurt him terribly and make him despise her—for his own sake. Now you have *Camille*, or *La Traviata*, one of the best, most tragic, and most dramatic plot structures ever devised (which is why that story will live forever and why there are so many bad imitations of it).

Take another trite plot-theme: the woman who sells herself to a man she does not love for the sake of the man whom she does love. Usually, as in the opera *Tosca*, some villain who knows of her love tells her that if she sleeps with him, he will spare her lover. The heroine makes the sacrifice and then has to hide the fact from her lover. This is a good, but simple, one-line conflict.

Now ask yourself how one can make it harder for the characters. Suppose the woman sells herself, not to a villain who forces her into it, but to a man who really loves her, whom she respects and whose love she takes seriously. He does not want to buy her, and she must hide from him that it is a sale—but she has to sell herself to save the man she really loves, a man who happens to be the particular person the buyer hates most. This is a much more dramatic conflict—and it is the plot-theme of *We the Living*.

I have asked myself: How can I make the conflict worse for everyone involved? By complicating the conflict, I have made a standard theme original.

The more conflicts involved in the same action situation, and the more serious the values for the participants, the better the dramatic situation and the tighter the plot you can construct from it.

Once an author starts to *develop* his plot-theme, he has to make the events proceed from that plot-theme. For instance, in *Notre-Dame de Paris*, the priest has the girl arrested and condemned to death, then offers her escape if she will give herself to him. This is a dramatization in action of the plot-theme conflict. Suppose the priest was not instrumental in having the girl arrested, but merely stood on the sidelines and wanted to help her escape from jail in order to have an affair with her. That would not be a plot structure (and three quarters of the book's drama would be lost).

In the novel, the hoboes of Paris attempt to rescue the girl from the cathedral of Notre-Dame, which they besiege. One of their leaders is the priest's young brother, a dissolute, useless playboy, representing the complete opposite of the priest's ideals, but his only human value on earth besides the girl. In a horrible scene, Quasimodo, the priest's protégé, seizes this boy by the legs and cracks his skull against the façade of the cathedral.

If there had been no younger brother, the priest's conflict of values, and his tragedy, would have been lesser. And while the siege of the cathedral would still have had a certain plot value—the suspense of: "Will the heroine escape or not?"—that incident becomes much more dramatic when it involves a dramatic loss to the priest.

Every incident of *Notre-Dame de Paris* is ruled by the same principle: make it as hard as possible for the characters, and tie the lesser characters' tragedies to the main line of events. The best example is the story of the girl's mother, an old recluse whose only desire is to find her daughter, who was stolen by the Gypsies years ago. The woman hates all Gypsies, the heroine in particular. At the end, in the climax, by seizing the girl's arm, she delays her long enough so that the soldiers pursuing her are able to find her—and in that moment she discovers that the girl is her daughter. Why is it dramatic? Hugo selects the worst conflict possible for both the old woman and the girl: in that moment, nothing worse could have happened to them than to discover each other in such a manner.

This subplot is not involved in or essential to the plot-theme; but Hugo quite properly introduced it, in developing the story, since he could integrate it to the main line of events. By contrast, if the old mother had *not* served a plot purpose in the climax, she would have been irrelevant to and improper in the story.

At the end, the priest and Quasimodo watch the girl's execution from the tower of the cathedral. If the priest had leaned forward too far and fallen off the tower, that would have been a disastrous anticlimax; it would have been completely purposeless, and therefore meaningless. But what did Hugo, the dramatist, do? Quasimodo, the devoted protégé, sees the priest gloating over the execution and pushes him over the side of the tower. *That* is a resolution in action of their conflict of values.

The scene that follows, in which the priest is caught on a water-spout and hangs over the pavement, is magnificently dramatic. It is a physical illustration of the novel's central conflict, and of its resolution: the girl is being executed on the square below; Quasimodo is standing above, crying; the priest hangs between life and death in sheer horror, and finally crashes to punishment.

This is one of the most satisfying resolutions in literature (speaking only in terms of dramatic values, which one judges by the nature of the conflict the author has set up). Hugo's skill is such that he does not let the priest die immediately, without knowing the nature of his punishment. The priest lives long enough to know—his soul (and thus the reader's soul) realizes consciously for a few minutes the spiritual meaning of the whole central conflict.

If you understand the mechanics of what makes this good, you understand the essence of plot construction.

In reading *Notre-Dame de Paris*, one feels interest, tension, horror. Watch for the means by which these ends are achieved, and, underlying the writing style, you will see the skeleton of the plot structure, which in turn is determined by the plot-theme. Those scenes at the end of the novel hold your attention because they are the logical resolution of the central conflict, the same conflict by which the author has held you up to this point. If the final scenes had come out of nowhere, they would not have held you.

Of course, the author has to be a good stylist to write the scenes properly; but style is a secondary issue. The best style in the world will not save a plotless story. You might say of it: "That's a lovely way of using words"—but nothing more. The power of the climax of *Notre-Dame de Paris* comes from the combination of good writing and that which *makes* the writing good: the magnificent plot structure, magnificently resolved.

Now I want to clarify the difference between drama and melodrama.

A drama involves primarily a conflict of values *within* a man (as expressed in action); a melodrama involves only conflicts of a man with other men. (These are my own definitions. Dictionaries usually define melodrama as "exaggerated drama," which is not a proper definition because it leaves open the question of what is or is not exaggerated.)

Conflict with other men is the pattern of detective stories and Westerns, where two sides who have nothing in common are set against each other by their opposition of interests—as when a detective pursues a criminal. There *is* conflict, and a good plot can be built from it, but all the danger is physical and external. The detective has only one aim: to catch the criminal; and the criminal only one aim: to escape. The sole line of interest is: Who will outsmart whom? There is no real drama, only the drama of action.

But suppose the detective learns that the criminal is his own son. Then he is caught between his love for the son and his duty as a policeman. He has a spiritual conflict, a conflict of values *within* himself—and the story is lifted from detective fiction into drama.

My heroes in *The Fountainhead* and *Atlas Shrugged*, Roark and Galt, hold no contradictory values; it is through their friends, or the woman they love, that they are put into inner conflicts. The main line of the inner conflict of each concerns his (proper) love for a woman who, having not yet reached his level, is in some way still tied to the conventional world. Through her, the hero is thrown into conflict with a world *in which he now has something at stake*. In the case of Roark and Dominique, the fault is Dominique's; she is guilty of holding a mistaken, though not irrational, philosophy. Once she comes to hold the right philosophy, there is no clash, and the hero's two values, love and career, coincide. (What if the hero fell in love with an irrational woman who never corrected her views? A rational man would not do that, or not for long. When he grasped the woman's irrationality, he would feel no love.)

This illustrates my premise that evil is impotent. It is only the good that (if mistaken) can hurt the good. As Galt tells Dagny in *Atlas Shrugged*: "My actual enemies are of no danger to me. *You* are."

In *The Fountainhead*, Roark's struggle for his career is not yet drama; it is really melodrama. He struggles for his values, and society opposes him in the name of opposite values. But his relationship with Dominique or Wynand or Cameron—his struggle for the souls of those people who are between himself and society—that is drama.

In any properly constructed story of someone's struggle against society, the elements of drama—of an *inner* conflict of values—always involve those people who are partly in both camps. The drama comes from the hero's concern with the fate of those souls who are torn between his world and an alien world.

The physical events of *Notre-Dame de Paris* are of the kind that today would be called rank melodrama, but they are actually drama since they are motivated by inner spiritual conflicts. For instance, if someone falls from a building, hangs for a moment on a pole over the street, and then crashes to his death, this has a certain physical suspense. Hugo makes the same kind of event spiritual and dramatic, rather than melodramatic. Or take a standard device of melodrama: a girl tied to the railroad tracks, with the train about to run her over. If villains put her there, this is melodrama. But suppose that, for some reason, the man she loves put her there. Even though the physical action is rather crude, I would then classify it as drama.

In *Atlas Shrugged*, I deliberately use the standard devices of melodrama for a spiritual purpose. To end a part with the heroine crashing in an airplane, leaving the reader in suspense about her fate, is the kind of melodramatic device that would have been used in old movie serials (and that I would have liked even as melodrama, because there *is* the drama of physical action). But when one adds the spiritual significance—when one knows whom the heroine of *Atlas Shrugged* is pursuing and why she is in that position—then her crashing in an airplane is drama. The same applies to the last chapter of the novel, where Ragnar Danneskjöld flies through a window in order to rescue Galt. If no spiritual values had been involved beyond a rescue, this would have been melodrama. But when such a physical action is tied to serious, important values, it is drama.

In this sense, I believe with Victor Hugo that the more melodramatic the action in which one can express the drama, the better the story. (By "melodramatic" I here mean physical danger or action.) If you can unite the two—if you can give a relevant and logical physical expression to the spiritual conflict you present—then you have high-class drama.

One could conceivably write a story in which a man struggles against nothing but himself, i.e., in which the only conflict is within the man, and the other characters are passive. The actions he would take in pursuit of one of his values versus the other would create a logical plot progression. He could be torn between two women, one representing sacred love and the other profane; and he could get himself into very dramatic situations where the two women would be not his antagonists, but only his foils, against whom or for whom he takes the actions. Such a story would be marvelous to write. But I have never seen it done, and technically it would be difficult to do.

The usual pattern of drama is a conflict within the hero himself *and* a conflict against other men. This creates the best, most complex plot structures. For instance, when Rearden in *Atlas Shrugged* hesitates between quitting his job and continuing the struggle, this is a conflict against outside forces. At the same time, his love for Dagny is in conflict with what he thinks is his duty to his wife. This is an inner conflict which complicates his struggle against the outside world, ultimately causing him to almost lose that struggle.

The important thing here is integration. Suppose Rearden's romantic conflict had nothing to do with his economic conflict; one issue was private and the other public, and the two never met in the events of the story. Then the inclusion of both conflicts in the same story would be purely coincidental, and the plot would be badly constructed.

To create a plot structure, in sum, you must begin with a conflict; but not every conflict is sufficient for constructing a novel. Many conflicts are "one-incident" conflicts; they are too simple and, therefore, too easily resolved to permit a complex development. They might be good for a short story, but nothing more.

A short story, being of limited length, should properly deal only with a single incident—some one problem set up and resolved, without too many complications. To string out a whole series of incidents in the course of a short story makes for a bad story—a mere synopsis of something that should have been longer.

By contrast, a novel necessarily deals with a *series* of events. It may be constructed around the events of a single day, but then, by means of flashbacks or otherwise, the events are extended into a complex structure.

A novelette is an in-between form, with length as the attribute which distinguishes it from a novel or a short story. A novelette, like a novel, can have more than a single incident, as *Anthem* does. *Anthem* presents a long series of incidents—in an abbreviated, essentialized, almost "impressionistic" form. On the other hand, a single-incident story might require so many details in the telling that it becomes a novelette.

Your central conflict must be complex enough to warrant the development of events on the scale you intend. If you want to write a novel, your plot-theme has to be a much more complicated conflict than what would suffice for a short story.

A plot-theme is a conflict in terms of action, complex enough to create a purposeful progression of events. If you recall that this last is the definition of plot, you will see that the plot-theme serves as the seed from which the tree has to grow. To test whether you have sufficient seed for a good tree, ask yourself: Is this the worst situation in which I can put my hero? If these are his values, is this the worst clash I can engineer between them?

If you have chosen the worst clash possible, and if the values are important, you have a good seed for a good plot structure.

5

The Climax

The climax is that event or development within a story where all the struggles of the characters are resolved. Naturally, it comes near the end; how near depends on the nature of the story. Sometimes the climax is the very last event; usually, however, a few closing events are needed to show the consequences of the resolution.

For instance, the climax of *We the Living* is the scene where Andrei discovers that Kira is Leo's mistress, and, as part of the same development, Andrei's speech to the Party, when he rebels openly. The events which follow are merely the conclusion.

The climax of *The Fountainhead* is the Cortlandt explosion and Roark's trial.

The main issues of *The Fountainhead* were the following: the conflict of Roark against society; the conflict of Roark against Dominique, who believed that the good cannot win on earth—that evil is powerful and will always win; the conflict of Roark against Wynand, who believed that the pursuit of power (the power to rule men by force) is a practical means of serving his own idealistic values; the contrast between Roark and Keating, the originator versus the second-hander who attempts to rise by using other people rather than his own mind; the conflict of Roark against Toohey, the man deliberately committed to an evil philosophy of power.

The explosion of the Cortlandt housing project resolves all of these issues.

The Cortlandt explosion (and aftermath) shows us Roark winning against society. It brings Dominique back to Roark by convincing her that the good does win, regardless of how terrible its struggle against evil is. When Wynand attempts to defend Roark in the Cortlandt case, he comes to realize that his whole life policy is mistaken, that the kind of power he has sought—power over men—can only destroy his values, not serve them. The Cortlandt project is the climax of Keating's lifelong attempt to rise as a second-hander—and the final act of his hopeless destruction. As to Toohey, he is at the height of his power, he mobilizes all the collective forces of public opinion that he can in the Cortlandt case—and he loses.

This is the pattern of a complex *plot* climax—a climax in action, not merely in discussion. I had to devise an action that dramatized and resolved all of the above conflicts (and many smaller ones), showing in each case which side wins, which one loses, and why. Not every novel is as complex as *The Fountainhead*, but if you understand the method by which all its conflicts were integrated in its climax, you will be able to construct climaxes for stories of your own, which might involve fewer issues.

(On a first novel, I do not advise that you try anything as complex as *The Fountainhead*. But there are no "shoulds" in a literary career. If you feel you can, go right ahead.)

The climax is that stage at which the worst consequences of the plot-theme conflict come into the open and the characters have to make their final choice. You can judge a story's climax by asking: Has it resolved the central conflict? If not, the story is badly constructed.

If you know the plot-theme of your story, you will know what is the proper climax, and whether or not you are letting your story down. If the central conflict merely peters out—or if it is resolved unclearly, so that the reader does not really know what final decisions the characters have made—this is an improper ending.

A climax does not have to take place in one day or one scene. There is no rule about its length, which is determined by the nature of the story and by the number of issues which have to be resolved. In a stage play, the climax usually does take place in one scene; in a novel, it can involve several events. But these events have to be part of *one sequence*. For instance, the Cortlandt explosion and Roark's trial are several chapters apart; but all the events in this part of the story are intrinsically connected. The explosion sets off the climax, and the other events—such as Toohey's activity, Wynand's failure, Roark's trial and victory—follow from or are involved in this one action.

The term *anticlimax* refers to a development after the climax that does not follow from it. For instance, it would have been an anticlimax if, after the Cortlandt trial, I had shown Roark and Wynand quarreling about an unpaid commission on some building. Considering the issues that had been resolved between them, such an issue could be of no importance. Its only function would be to destroy the importance of the climax.

Never resolve a smaller issue after the climax. In a story with multiple threads, the problems of the lesser characters, if not involved in the climax, have to be solved before the climax. An example is the subplot of Irina and Sasha in *We the Living*. It would have been a bad anticlimax had I shown their fate—their being sent to Siberia and their parting—after I had shown Kira shot on the border. Or, in *The Fountainhead*, the romance of Keating and Katie was important throughout the story, and some conclusion to it had to be reached. But it would have been improper to show their last meeting after Dominique's ride to Roark at the top of the Wynand building.

It is important, however, that every conflict be resolved before the story ends. An annoying aspect of badly constructed novels is that the author often poses minor problems and then leaves them hanging in the air, as if he has forgotten all about them. (Of course, in really bad novels, even the major issues are not resolved.) In this regard, Chekhov had a good rule, which applies just as much to novels as to plays: "Never hang a gun on the wall in the first act if you don't intend to have it go off in the third." This applies to everything in a plot structure. (The breach of this rule is called a "red herring.")

When you construct a plot, the first event to figure out is always the climax. Suppose you have an idea for the theme and subject of a story but have not yet invented the climax. Then do not start to outline the story from the beginning. If you set up a lot of interesting conflicts and seemingly connected events without knowing where you are going, and then attempt to devise a climax that resolves it all, the process will be an excruciating mental torture (and you will not succeed). Therefore, in planning your story, get to your climax as quickly as possible. First devise an event that dramatizes and resolves the issues of your story, then construct the rest of the plot backward, by asking yourself what events are needed in order to *bring* your characters to this point.

This is a good example of the process of final causation. In order to judge what incidents to include in your story, you have to know your purpose in the story—i.e., your climax. Only when you know this can you begin to analyze which steps, each serving as the efficient cause of the next, will lead your characters logically to this decisive event.

There is no rule about what element has to be the first germ of a story in your mind. Fortunate writers are sometimes able to devise the climax first; in other words, they get a dramatic idea that constitutes the climax of a story, then work backward to construct the plot (which is sheer pleasure). This is a matter of pure accident. What *kind* of story you will tell is not an accident; it depends on your premises. But whether you first think of a character and then add the other elements, or of an abstract theme, or of a conflict situation—that is accidental. You are free to start at any point, because no matter where you start, you have to complete the circle and include all the other elements.

The only rule is that you have to know your climax (in dramatized terms) before you start to outline the steps by which to arrive there.

It has been said that Broadway is full of first acts. Many people can come up with an intriguing first act but do not know what to do with the play thereafter. By contrast, a good dramatist starts with the third act. He does not necessarily *write* the third act, or the climax, first—but he keeps it in mind.

I once asked a woman writer of lending-library fiction about her method of writing, and she answered airily: "Oh, I throw a bunch of characters up in the air and let them come down." Her stories read like it. This is a horrible example of what *not* to do.

In the same school are those modern writers who start with some assignment such as "a mood of adolescence" or "my search for the meaning of life in prep school." When they write, the standard of selection is the mood of the moment. The result is the kind of story where you do not know why one incident was included rather than another, or what is the purpose of it all. Behind such a hodgepodge is always a writer who starts without a defined plan and then writes as his feelings dictate.

The best metaphor for the relationship of an outline to a story is blueprints in relationship to a building. Nobody can start piling up girders or making window trimmings without a blueprint; a blueprint is necessary in order to judge what are the stresses and strains, and what to put where. The same is true of the construction of a story.

If you can carry the outline in your mind, you do not have to write it down, but it is helpful to do so if the story is complex. You might hold a story in your mind in a generalized way and think it is all in order; yet when you put it down on paper, you might discover dull stretches in which nothing in particular happens, or omissions of elements necessary to make later events dramatic.

By writing down the outline, I do not mean writing a synopsis in objective terms that an outsider would understand. I make my outlines as brief as possible, in what I call "headline style." For instance, the events that finally went into *Atlas Shrugged* were all present in my outline, but in this form: "[Chapter I] 'Who is John Galt?' Eddie Willers, Taggart Transcontinental, James Taggart. Trouble on the Colorado line. Taggart's evasions."* When I write an outline, I know more specifically than this what will go under the general headings, but I write down only what I need in order to remember the progression and to get a bird's-eye view of the structure

There is no rule about how detailed or concise to make your outline. Train yourself to know how much you can carry in your head, and how much you need to write down in order to see the total and keep the structure of your story clear in your mind.

When you come to the actual writing, there is no rule which demands that you have to write from the first chapter onward. If

*See David Harriman, ed., *Journals of Ayn Rand* (New York: Dutton, 1997), pp. 532–40.

your outline is good and you know where you are going, the order of execution is optional. Some writers write the end first, or any scene which they particularly want to write. This is permissible provided they are skillful enough to hide the seams—i.e., provided they can edit and integrate the total so that it reads as if the writer had started from the beginning.

I myself always start at the beginning. I can make notes on scenes, or on dialogue, in advance, but I cannot do the actual writing out of sequence; I deal with such complex issues that too much in each scene depends on what has been established earlier. If I started to concretize something in the middle while the concretes of the beginning were not firmly set in my mind, I would never be able to integrate the total or to write any scene properly.

There is another reason why I cannot write out of sequence, even on a simple story like *Anthem*. I am always very aware of what has gone before. One of my methods is to have plants in the course of a story, on which I play later; i.e., I have references in later scenes to something that was established earlier. For instance, at the end of *Atlas Shrugged*, Eddie Willers is suddenly talking to Dagny [in his imagination], addressing a memory of their childhood that was planted in the first chapter. When I wrote that particular passage in the first chapter, eleven years before I came to the end, I knew that I was planting it for this purpose. I did the same with Halley's Fifth Concerto: the description of it in the first chapter of *Atlas Shrugged* is copied verbatim in the last. When the reader comes to it the second time, the same words have acquired a much fuller meaning. In the first chapter, they are a generalized emotional abstraction; by the end, they are a philosophical-emotional summation of the ideas of the story.

Planting those small touches in a scene to cash in on them later is a personal preference of mine. Every good writer does not necessarily do it, and I mention it here only as one reason why I prefer to write from the beginning onward. But that is not an absolute rule.

The only absolute rule is that, whether you write from the beginning or the end or the middle, you must start *plotting* from the end.

6

How to Develop a Plot Ability

You have heard it said that "art cannot be taught." There *is* a sense in which writing cannot be taught; but in a different sense, it can.

To learn sciences like physics or history is simply to absorb facts consciously. Such sciences can be taught since the facts involved can be communicated. Physical skills like typing can also be taught. But to learn to type, more is required than merely listening to a factual lecture: you have to practice. First you learn how to move your fingers and strike the keys—slowly and by conscious effort. Learning to type then consists of automatizing this skill.

At first you have to think of how to crook your fingers, how far to reach for each letter, how to keep in tempo. Then you practice, faster and faster, so that eventually, when you look at a page of copy which you have to type, your fingers do the rest "instinctively." If an experienced typist were to ask herself, "How do I do it?" she would answer, "I just do it."

The same is true of dancing, or playing tennis, or any physical skill. First it is learned consciously—and you are in command of the skill when it becomes automatic, so that conscious attention is no longer required.

I pause on this analysis in order to illustrate what kind of automatic "instincts" have to be acquired in the realm of art.

I mentioned earlier the complexity involved in writing a single sentence [see pp. 1–2]. I said that you could not figure out the sentence consciously. You sit down to write, the sentence comes out a certain way, and with editing you can improve it—but you cannot compose the sentence consciously in the way that you can pass an examination in physics by stating the facts as you have learned and understood them.

This is why the process of writing cannot be taught—not because it is a mystical talent, but because so complex an integration is involved that no teacher can supervise the process for you. You can learn all the theory, but unless you practice—unless you actually write—you will not be able to apply the theory.

All that a teacher can do is explain the elements of writing and suggest a method of thinking and practicing that will enable you to write. I cannot give you rules sufficient to make you wake up one day with a talent for plot. But you *can* acquire such a talent if you know some general rules and the kind of mental exercises that will integrate into a plot ability.

So let me give you a few general rules for conditioning your plot imagination.

Concretize Your Abstractions

One rule that you need both as a human being and as a fiction writer is: Concretize your abstractions.

In your daily life, in thinking, and in reading, you deal constantly with wide abstractions. If you have only a general idea of how to concretize these, they are "floating abstractions." If you can name one or two concretes under some concept, but no more, it is a semifloating abstraction. You do have some knowledge of how it applies to reality, but your understanding is very limited. For instance, if you are asked what you mean by "independence," and you say, "A man who thinks for himself," that is one good concrete. Much more is necessary, however, in order to understand such an abstraction as "independence."

If you catch yourself using floating or semifloating abstractions, learn to concretize them. Project in ultimate action what any abstraction means.

For instance, it is worthless to say: "Love, well, everybody knows what love is." To bring it down to earth, you might first say: "Love is a human emotion of appreciation for a value." This is a good philosophical definition, but it is not yet concrete. To make it concrete, you must project what it means to observe love. Not only: How does it feel? but: How do you know it in other people? A writer has to project his abstractions in specific concretes. That he knows something inwardly is not enough; he has to make the reader know it; and the reader can grasp it only from the outside, by some physical means. Concretize to yourself: If a man and a woman are in love, how do they act? what do they say? what do they seek? why do they seek it? That is the concrete reality, for which "love" is merely a wide abstraction.

You do not have to start concretizing all your concepts systematically. Start with those which interest you most, or proceed at random, whenever you catch yourself using a floating abstraction. Do it whenever your mind is unemployed, on the bus or while brushing your teeth. Train your mind to concretize every abstraction as a general policy. As with typing, it is only at first that you have to do it by conscious, measured steps. Eventually it becomes an automatic mental habit.

(I recommend that you start with those abstractions all writers deal with but few understand fully in concrete terms—i.e., all abstractions which pertain to emotions, values, virtues, and actions. Most intelligent adults think they understand the abstractions that relate to human beings—love, hate, fear, anger, independence or dependence, selfishness or unselfishness—but if they try, they cannot easily reduce them to concrete reality.)

Not to carry floating abstractions in your mind is the first requisite for inventing a plot—because action is concrete and physical. Abstractions do not act.

Once you can relate every abstraction to its concretes, you will know how to translate general themes into action. Any theme that you want to write a story about starts in your mind (once you name it) as an abstraction. To translate that abstraction into a plot, you need a vast number of concretes at your "instinctive" call so that your subconscious can pick the relevant ones.

For instance, to present a conflict between individualism and collectivism, you must have stored away countless concretes under those abstractions—in the personal, political, and philosophical realms. From these stored concretes, your subconscious can then select and integrate events that dramatize your theme. You will not have to figure out by conscious effort: "Roark is an individualist, so of course he wouldn't do a housing project; but maybe he would—under what conditions? Well, what *would* an individualist do and what is 'individualism'?"

I did not go through this latter process; instead, the idea for the climax of *The Fountainhead* hit me like Newton's apple. One day, during lunch—I can remember where and in what drugstore—when I was thinking of the climax, the idea for the housing project suddenly flashed into my mind. But "accidents happen only to those who deserve them." In other words, the idea came to me because I had done an enormous amount of thinking while working on the outline and theme of *The Fountainhead* (and long before).

This kind of incident is what makes nonintrospective writers say: "Ah, writing is a mystical talent—it just comes to me." By contrast, since I am a good introspector, I can tell exactly how these things happen. I cannot tell what subconscious connections are made in my mind preceding the moment an idea strikes. But I do know that the subconscious works somewhat like a [computer]. If you feed it the right data and ask the right question, it gives you the answer. You do not have to know how the wires connect inside.

Fill your subconscious with as many concretes as possible under every abstraction you deal with—then forget about them. Your subconscious does not forget. The concretes will be there when, dealing with some complex theme and needing a complex integration, you press the buttons of your [computer]: "I need a climax that resolves issue X, problem Y." Your thought here is a series of abstractions. If these are fully in your control—if they are not merely floating abstractions without content—your subconscious makes the connections and gives you the answer (sooner or later, depending on the complexity of the problem).

You must be able to work backward and forward from the abstract to the concrete. In other words, you must be able to concretize any abstraction you deal with and, vice versa, to draw the abstraction from any *concretes* you deal with.

Train yourself to see what any series of concretes—whether people, events, character traits, or whatever—have in common. "I have seen a number of people do X. The premise behind it is Y." When you think like this, you are abstracting a concept or a general principle from a number of concretes.

If you do not constantly draw abstractions of your own, you lose a lot of good material. For instance, you might observe some characteristic thing that people do which would be good to include in your writing. But if you store it in your subconscious without tying it to anything else, it is lost. It is only a concrete observation and will be of no value to you.

Instead, tie your observations to abstractions. For instance, you observe that someone is aggressive in a nasty way, and that he is also frightened and uncertain. You might conclude that he is putting on a show, that he is a coward who is aggressive as a defense. This is classifying a concrete under an abstraction—and this is the kind of observation that will be valuable to you as a writer.

When you master the relationship of abstractions to concretes, you will know how to translate an abstract theme into action, and how to attach an abstract meaning to an action idea. If you start with a philosophical abstraction, you will be able to translate it into a conflict, a climax, and a plot. Or if you get a plot idea which at first glance has no philosophical meaning, you will be able to discover the meaning and develop the idea into a serious story.

If you have to crank the process by hand because you have not yet mastered the abstract-concrete relationship, it will take forever and seem impossible. Only when your mind is geared to dancing back and forth—and I mean *dance,* with that kind of ease—between abstractions and concretes will you be able to give the philosophical meaning to an action idea or the action story to a philosophical idea.

Plot action is not mere physical action, and it is not mere spiritual or mental action. Some writers think that if a man takes a trip and comes home, this constitutes plot action (he *did* something!), just as the writers of bad melodramas think it is plot action if someone is chasing someone and there is five minutes of speeding cars or horses galloping. The counterpart of this error is conflicts within a man's mind which are not illustrated in physical action.

The arty, modern stream-of-consciousness novels, on the one hand, and bad melodramas on the other, where characters run around hectically, are two versions of the same error. (The latter is action—so why is it so dull? It is dull because it is *mere* physical action.) Proper plot action is neither spirit alone nor body alone, but the integration of the two, with the physical action expressing the spiritual action involved.

To construct a proper plot, you have to be (at least as a dramatist) on the premise of mind-body integration. If to any extent you hold the premise of a mind-body split, it will hamper your plot ability, because it will lead you to consider dramatic the mere fact that a man experiences something in his own mind, or that he moves around in some mindless physical action.

A story is like a soul-body relationship. Whether you start with the body (the action) or the soul (the abstract theme), you must be able to integrate the two. And the proper integration of idea to action requires a mind that is not confined to thinking merely in terms of physical concretes, or merely in terms of floating abstractions.

Think in Terms of Conflict

A proper plot situation involves a conflict of values. Therefore, the next point—the real fiction writer's point—is: Learn to think in terms of conflict.

A valuable exercise is the following. When you go to modern movies, watch television shows, or read modern novels, which with rare exceptions are plotless (or have inept plots), try to correct them mentally. If a story begins interestingly but then peters out, see what you could have done with that beginning, how you could have turned that story into a real conflict of important values. You will encounter such wasted opportunities in almost every modern story (although some are no good even for this purpose because they lack any rudiments of a plot).

I am not recommending plagiarism. I recommend this only as a mental exercise, only as training in how to give a purposeful plot structure to some shapeless presentation of undefined events and people. And the lead to doing it is: Think in terms of conflict.

At the start of my career, I had a valuable conversation with Cecil DeMille. It was my first year in Hollywood, I was twenty-two, and I had already developed a strong plot sense; but although I could recognize a good plot story, I had not consciously identified what characteristics made it good. DeMille told me something that clarified the issue for me.

He said that a good story depends on what he called "the situation," by which he meant a complicated conflict [a plot-theme], and that the best stories are those which can be told in one sentence. In other words, if the essential situation (not the whole story, of course) can be told in one sentence, this makes for a good plot story.

He told me how he happened to buy the story for one of his most successful silent-day pictures, *Manslaughter*. It was originally a novel, and a friend of his wired him in Hollywood advising him to buy it for the screen. The friend included only one sentence about the story: "A righteous young district attorney has to prosecute the woman he loves, a spoiled heiress, for killing a policeman in an automobile accident." This is all DeMille knew about the story, and he bought it.

This kind of sentence contains all the elements of a good story—because it gives you the conflict. Once you have this much, you can tell what kind of events you must construct in order to *lead* the characters to the setup, and what kind of events are its possible *consequences*. You will not grasp all the events immediately, a great many choices are involved—but you see the possibility of a dramatically constructed progression.

Anyone starting with this kind of idea is safe dramatically. It would take a bad writer to ruin it.

This is what you must aim at. Learn how to construct this type of situation, whether on your own or as you read plotless books or watch plotless television and movies. That will be your first and probably your most important step toward becoming a plot writer.

Tap Your Emotions

When you try to imagine events, ask yourself what kind of thing *you* would like to see happen.

The preceding leads have been technical; this one is emotional. You must start with the abstract idea of a conflict, but thereafter your own values and your personal imagination will be a reliable dramatic selector. Ask yourself, therefore, what kind of conflicts and events *you* would find interesting. You will be surprised at how productive this is.

When you ask this question, do not censor yourself or check yourself against your moral code. Simply tap your emotions; you can judge later whether they are right or wrong. Take yourself selfishly as the one who has to enjoy the spectacle of your story's events. Do not ask what kind of events would make the best propaganda, or what kind your potential audience might like—no, ask what you personally would like to see happen.

That is the best springboard for inventing events.

7

Characterization

Characterization is the presentation of the nature of the people in a story.

Characterization is really the presentation of *motives*. We understand a person if we understand what makes him act the way he does. To know a person well is to know "what makes him tick," as opposed to not seeing beyond the superficial actions of the moment.

The main means of characterization are *action* and *dialogue*—just as it is only by means of their actions and words that one can observe the characters of other people in real life. There is no way to know the soul (the consciousness) of another except by means of physical manifestations: his actions and words (not his words in the sense of philosophical declarations, but his words in the context of his actions). The same applies to fiction. As part of characterization, a writer can sum up in narrative passages a character's thoughts or feelings, but *merely* to do that is not characterization.

The actions that a writer shows must be integrated to his understanding of the characters' motives—which the reader then grasps by means of these actions. I have talked about the same kind of circle in relation to plot: to project an abstract theme, you must devise the concrete events from which the reader will in turn derive that theme. The same applies to characterization: to project a convincing character, you need to have an idea of the basic premises or motives which move his actions—and by means of these actions, the reader will discover what is at the root of the character.

The reader can then say: "This action is consistent, but that action is not." He can say it on the grounds of what the actions presented have implied about the character's motives.

This does not mean that you must present every character in a single key, giving him only one attribute or passion. It means that you must *integrate* a character. A character comes across as an integrated person when everything he says and does is internally consistent.

I want to emphasize that a character can have enormous conflicts and contradictions—but then *these* have to be consistent. You must select his actions so that the reader grasps: "*This* is what's the trouble with this character." For instance, there are contradictions in Gail Wynand's actions throughout *The Fountainhead*, but these contradictions are integrated to their ultimate root. If a character has contradictory premises, to say "I understand him" means: "I understand the conflict behind his actions."

When a character "does not jell," it means that the evidence offered about him is never unified, neither into one whole nor into a comprehensible conflict.

In Sinclair Lewis's *Arrowsmith*, the hero is supposed to be a medical scientist of unusual stature; yet one is never convinced of his actual devotion to science.

The reader meets him first as a boy: "Cross-legged in the examining-chair in Doc Vickerson's office, a boy was reading 'Gray's Anatomy.' His name was Martin Arrowsmith. . . . By sheer brass and obstinacy he had, at fourteen, become the unofficial, also decidedly unpaid, assistant to the Doc." For a boy of that age to want to work in a doctor's office is unusual, and it might indicate a budding passion for medicine. But observe the next touch. In the office stands "a skeleton with one gaunt gold tooth. On evenings when the Doc was away, Martin would acquire prestige among [his friends] by leading them into the unutterable darkness and scratching a sulfur match on the skeleton's jaw."

I submit that this touch alone destroys the earnestness of the character.

It is quite possible that a devoted crusader of science might in childhood have pulled such a stunt—as a prank of the moment, meaning nothing in particular. But when you draw a character, everything that you say about him acquires significance by the mere fact of being included in your story. Art is *selectivity*. You cannot re-create every minute detail about anything, neither about an event nor about a person; therefore, that which you choose to include, or to omit, is significant—and you have to watch carefully the implications of what you say or omit. If you introduce a boy as seriously interested in medicine and then show him playing silly, childish pranks, the earnestness of his devotion is immediately undercut.

The subsequent treatment of Arrowsmith follows the same pattern. His devotion to science in his college years is presented almost apologetically, in fragmentary bits (the author's tone being one of friendly, patronizing amusement). On the other hand, his social relationships and his feelings toward his fraternity are shown in great detail. He is presented as an average boy; apart from the fact that he takes medicine seriously while others take it lightly, he is given no character trait that separates him from others. He's just one of the boys.

I question the idea that a man with a great passion for science (as Arrowsmith is later shown to have) would be "one of the boys" in college. Any man with a serious central ambition is more of an outsider in his youth than in later years. It is particularly in his youth that he will be misunderstood and resented by others.

The attempt to make Arrowsmith a regular fellow, and to separate his private and social life from his attitude toward science, undercuts his characterization. Except for a few scenes dealing specifically with medicine, the reader at no point feels the presence of any driving force in the man.

Throughout Arrowsmith's later career, and throughout his romantic life, we see a man who blunders helplessly. His main actions do carry him toward his major love, which is the pursuit of pure science. But there are passages where he says, in effect: "To hell with science. I guess I'll be a small-town doctor and make money." Then he is drawn back to science. One might say: Here is a man who is struggling with the decision of whether or not to devote himself to science. But the unanswered question is: Why is he struggling in this manner? Why the doubts? How are they to be reconciled with his strong basic premise?

Arrowsmith's fumbling helplessness in regard to everything except the laboratory is never integrated to his strengths as a crusading scientist. The two elements simply coexist in the character; they do not logically go together, nor are they in any real *conflict*. As a result, the characterization is out of focus. At the end of the novel, the reader does not have a clear idea of Arrowsmith's motive power—of what makes him tick.

By contrast, Leora, Arrowsmith's wife, is projected clearly. From the moment we first meet her, we know that she is a girl who faces life directly, is rational and brave, goes after what she wants, and states her desires openly. She is a very appealing, and consistent, character; she has a directness and simplicity about her that remains in all of the story's different circumstances (including some very complicated ones). The reader sees her ever more fully, but she never changes in essence.

Leora's actions are self-explanatory. From her introduction onward, the reader never has to wonder why she acts as she does. He feels: "It would be like her to do that." Why does he feel it? Because her every action, decision, and word is consistent with the way she has been introduced.

(The only exception is certain inexcusable lines of dialogue she is given to the effect that "I'm just a simple, ordinary woman." She is *not* an ordinary woman, but a true heroine; and I resent, philosophically, this manner of labeling a character. The fact that Leora is not an ambitious creator on her own does not make her "just a little woman." My guess is that Lewis himself felt that Leora was the opposite of an ordinary woman; that he rather liked her—and had to assure the reader that he was impersonal and "objective," by the Naturalistic standard. He in effect says: "Don't think this is anything much." To a Naturalist, nothing exists that is "anything much.")

You can project your character only by means of what you say on paper; but behind every line and action, there is much more than what you put in words. No action is taken in a vacuum, and an alert reader is automatically watching for the meaning of every line and action. He is constantly on the lookout: "I'm meeting a new character. What makes him tick?" He is constantly making lightning-like calculations: "What premise does this action come from? What is the motive of a man who does X? The character says Z. Why does he say it?"

In order to show how much is implied between the lines, I have rewritten a scene from *The Fountainhead*. It is the first scene between two of the major characters, Howard Roark and Peter Keating. Read first the dialogue of the original scene (I have omitted the descriptions), and then the rewritten version of the same scene. Watch for the means of characterization. What do you learn about the two men, and how do you learn it? What impression do you have of them, and what gave you that impression?*

[The scene takes place on the day Roark has been expelled from college and Keating has graduated with high honors.]

"Congratulations, Peter," said Roark.

"Oh . . . Oh, thanks . . . I mean . . . do you know or . . . Has mother been telling you?"

"She has."

"She shouldn't have!"

"Why not?"

"Look, Howard, you know that I'm terribly sorry about your being . . ."

"Forget it."

"I . . . there's something I want to speak to you about, Howard, to ask your advice. Mind if I sit down?"

"What is it?"

"You won't think that it's awful of me to be asking about my business, when you've just been . . . ?"

"I said forget about that. What is it?"

"You know, I've often thought that you're crazy. But I know that you know many things about it—architecture, I mean—which those fools never knew. And I know that you love it as they never will."

*I have included these two versions here, even though they are already in *The Romantic Manifesto* (in the essay "Basic Principles of Literature"), because Ayn Rand's analysis here is fuller.

"Well?"

"Well, I don't know why I should come to you, but—Howard, I've never said it before, but you see, I'd rather have your opinion on things than the Dean's—I'd probably follow the Dean's, but it's just that yours means more to me myself, I don't know why. I don't know why I'm saying this, either."

"Come on, you're not being afraid of me, are you? What do you want to ask about?"

"It's about my scholarship. The Paris prize I got."

"Yes?"

"It's for four years. But, on the other hand, Guy Francon offered me a job with him some time ago. Today he said it's still open. And I don't know which to take."

"If you want my advice, Peter, you've made a mistake already. By asking me. By asking anyone. Never ask people. Not about your work. Don't you know what you want? How can you stand it, not to know?"

"You see, that's what I admire about you, Howard. You always know."

"Drop the compliments."

"But I mean it. How do you always manage to decide?"

"How can you let others decide for you?"

Now read the *rewritten* version of the same scene:

"Congratulations, Peter," said Roark.

"Oh . . . Oh, thanks . . . I mean . . . do you know or . . . Has mother been telling you?"

"She has."

"She shouldn't have!"

"Oh well, I didn't mind it."

"Look, Howard, you know that I'm terribly sorry about your being expelled."

"Thank you, Peter."

"I . . . there's something I want to speak to you about, Howard, to ask your advice. Mind if I sit down?"

"Go right ahead. I'll be glad to help you, if I can."

"You won't think that it's awful of me to be asking about my business, when you've just been expelled?"

"No. But it's nice of you to say that, Peter. I appreciate it."

"You know, I've often thought that you're crazy."

"Why?"

"Well, the kind of ideas you've got about architecture—there's nobody that's ever agreed with you, nobody of importance, not the Dean, not any of the professors . . . and they know their business. They're always right. I don't know why I should come to you."

"Well, there are many different opinions in the world. What did you want to ask me?"

"It's about my scholarship. The Paris prize I got."

"Personally, I wouldn't like it. But I know it's important to you."

"It's for four years. But, on the other hand, Guy Francon offered me a job with him some time ago. Today he said it's still open. And I don't know which to take."

"If you want my advice, Peter, take the job with Guy Francon. I don't care for his work, but he's a very prominent architect and you'll learn how to build."

"You see, that's what I admire about you, Howard. You always know how to decide."

"I try my best."

"How do you do it?"

"I guess I just do it."

"But you see, I'm not sure, Howard. I'm never sure of myself. You always are."

"Oh, I wouldn't say that. But I guess I'm sure about my work."

The plot content is the same in the rewritten scene as in the original, but the characters are different. In particular, Roark is changed.

In the original scene, Roark is impervious to Keating's and the conventional world's view of his expulsion. "*'Has mother been telling you?' 'She has.' 'She shouldn't have!' 'Why not?'*" Keating thinks that his own triumph would hurt Roark on the day of Roark's expulsion. But Roark does not share this comparative standard; and at first he does not even understand it. His "*Why not?*" indicates the difference between his standards and Keating's better than any other answer could have done. Even if the reader does not pause to analyze that sentence, it conveys the complete directness of a man who in effect says: "What's your kind of triumph to me? My standards are different."

In the rewritten scene, Roark says: "*Oh well, I didn't mind it.*" He accepts the comparative standard and agrees (although in a generous manner) that his expulsion is a disaster and Keating's graduation a triumph.

If you approach writing a scene like this with the idea that your hero is an independent man but you have not identified the issue any more clearly, you might think: "He's a strong man, so he'll say: 'I didn't mind it.' " This is where you have to watch your implications. If he says, " I didn't mind it," that implies something specific about his basic premises and motivation. If he says, "Why not?" that implies something entirely different.

In the original scene, Roark is courteous but indifferent. Not only does he reject Keating's standards, he shows no desire to discuss them; although he will listen if Keating has something to say. When Keating says, "*There's something I want to speak to you about, Howard, to ask your advice. Mind if I sit down?*" Roark merely asks, "*What is it?*" He is courteous to Keating in a manner consistent with their difference of standards.

In the rewritten scene, Roark says: "*Go right ahead. I'll be glad to help you, if I can.*" Here he is courteous beyond politeness—he is actually interested. That is a contradiction, because it raises the question: Why, given their opposite standards, is he interested?

In the original scene, Roark at one point shows friendliness. Observe what that friendliness proceeds from. Keating says: "*Well, I don't know why I should come to you, but—Howard, I've never said it before, but you see, I'd rather have your opinion on things than the Dean's—I'd probably follow the Dean's, but it's just that yours means more to me myself, I don't know why. I don't know why I'm saying this, either.*" This is a speech of profound respect for Roark: Keating acknowledges the superiority of Roark's standards, and he shows sincerity. Roark can reward that with a moment of friendliness, which amounts to saying: "If this is how you feel, I can talk to you." Observe also the generous form of his friendliness. He says: "*You're not being afraid of me, are you?*" He knows that Keating *is* afraid of him, and to make the conversation easier for Keating, he acknowledges this openly.

I have seen young writers influenced by me make their hero a monotone. He speaks only in snappy yeses or noes, never shows anything but a tight grimness, and is always on the fighting premise. This is bad characterization; it is incomplete. The reader necessarily thinks: "A man cannot be this way *all* the time—nor can any man have only one premise."

Good characterization is not a matter of giving a character a single attribute or making him monotonous. It is a matter of integrating his every particular aspect to the total, the focus of integration being his basic premises. For instance, Roark is not only the man of integrity, fighting everybody. He can be friendly and charming; he can be generous; he even has a few humorous lines (though I think only two in the whole novel). He has all sorts of facets. But he comes across as a monolith because every facet is consistent with his basic premises.

The above example from the original scene is an illustration of this: Roark can be generous and friendly to Keating, but only in the context of Keating's acknowledging his, Roark's, premises.

In the *rewritten* scene, when Keating says, "*You won't think that it's awful of me to be asking about my business, when you've just been expelled?*" Roark answers, "*No. But it's nice of you to say that, Peter. I appreciate it.*" Here he shows friendliness in exchange, not for Keating's tribute to his standards, but for Keating's condolences on the bad state to which those standards have brought him. Instead of being a generous man extending a helping hand when deserved, he becomes a man accepting charity. In this context, Roark's friendliness acquires an entirely different meaning.

Again, if you approach a scene like this with the abstract intention "I will show my hero being friendly," but you have not concretized the nature of that friendliness or integrated it with your hero's other premises, you might commit a contradiction like the above and then wonder why your character does not come across as you intended.

In the rewritten scene, when Keating says, "*You know, I've often thought that you're crazy,*" Roark asks, "*Why?*" This shows concern for

Keating's opinion, and even self-doubt. In some other context where he had a reason to put Keating on the spot, Roark *could* have asked this question defiantly or sarcastically. But in the context of this scene, he accepts a gratuitous insult by saying, in effect: "Oh, you think I'm crazy. Why? Maybe I am."

In the original scene, Keating says: "*You know, I've often thought that you're crazy. But I know that you know many things about it—architecture, I mean—which those fools never knew. And I know that you love it as they never will.*" This shows what a context can do to a single line: accompanied by such an explanation, the statement "you're crazy" is a great compliment. But if Keating merely says, "*I've often thought that you're crazy,*" Roark should stop talking to him then and there—if he is the Roark intended originally.

In the original scene, when Keating finally asks his question, Roark takes his problem seriously and gives him advice, not about a concrete, but about the wider principle involved. "*If you want my advice, Peter, you've made a mistake already. By asking me. By asking anyone. Never ask people. Not about your work.*" Roark gives Keating the benefit of his own convictions, telling him that there is a more serious issue involved than merely the choice of the two possibilities. The line "*If you want my advice, Peter, you've made a mistake already*" is unexpected, arresting, and unconventional; and since Roark backs it up by giving his reasons, the reader not only sees the nature of Roark's premises, but also a boy who is thinking—and thinking in much wider terms than the particular choice of a job.

In the rewritten scene, Roark does the conventional thing: he gives Keating specific advice. This implies that there is nothing wrong in Keating's asking for such advice or following another man's opinion.

(In the book, Roark later gives Keating the same advice, but contemptuously and indifferently, simply to end the conversation. By that time, Keating's sincerity is gone; he is putting on an act for Roark; and Roark merely dismisses him. This again is an issue of the implications of a context.)

In the original scene, my best touch of characterization is the following exchange. Keating says, "*How do you always manage to decide?*" and Roark answers, "*How can you let others decide for you?*"

These two lines convey the essence of the two characters. In the rewritten scene, I dropped them.

I want to pause on these lines in order to show how to integrate philosophical propaganda into fiction.

Such an issue as "I always decide for myself" versus "I go by the opinions of others" is extremely wide. If two characters started discussing it out of a clear sky, that would be sheer propaganda. But in the above scene, the two men are stating an abstract issue as it applies to their own problems and to the concrete situation before the reader's eyes. The abstract discussion is natural in the context, and, therefore, almost unnoticeable.

This is the only way to state abstract principles in fiction. If the concrete illustration is given in the problems and actions of the story, you can afford to have a character state a wide principle. If, however, the action does *not* support it, that wide principle will stick out like a propaganda poster.

How much philosophy you can present without turning into a propagandist, as opposed to a proper fiction writer, depends on how much of an event the philosophy is covering. In the above scene, it would have been too early for the two boys to make more of a statement than they did, even though the issue stated is independence versus second-handedness, which is the theme of the whole book. Given what is specifically concretized in the scene, one exchange of lines is enough abstract philosophy.

A speech like John Galt's in *Atlas Shrugged* would have been too much for Roark's courtroom speech in *The Fountainhead*. The events of *The Fountainhead* do not illustrate as many issues as do the events of *Atlas Shrugged*.

To judge how long a philosophical speech should be, go by the following standard: How detailed and complex are the events which you have offered to concretize the speech? If the events warrant it, you can make as long a statement as you wish without taking the reader outside the framework of the story.

Now look again at the rewritten scene. I depart blatantly from the original Roark when he says: "*Well, there are many different opinions in the world.*" This implies a tolerant respect for all differences of opinion, and thus a nonobjective, nonabsolute view of ideas—as contrasted to such absolutism in the original scene that Roark does not even bother to argue about ideas with Keating.

Next, Keating says: "*You always know how to decide.*" Roark answers: "*I try my best.*" If you are presenting a man who is independent and who will go on to fight the whole world, and if in one of the first scenes he says, "*I try my best,*" you give yourself a handicap in characterization that no amount of heroic actions on your hero's part can overcome. It is a blatant contradiction: a strong man who relies only on his own judgment would never utter such a modest line.

Next, Keating asks: "*How do you do it?*" Roark answers: "*I guess I just do it.*" Journalistically, this line can pass almost unnoticed; that is the normal way for men of average premises to speak. But no heroic rebel, particularly not a representative of rationality, will ever say "*I guess I just do it*" about his own career.

Then Keating says: "*But you see, I'm not sure, Howard. I'm never sure of myself. You always are.*" Roark answers: "*Oh, I wouldn't say that. But I guess I'm sure about my work.*" This line characterizes Roark as a man who does not hold self-confidence as an absolute virtue; he sees no reason why he should be confident about anything except his work. The result is that he becomes superficial and concrete-bound. He might be principled in regard to his work, but he has no wider idea of principles, no basic philosophical convictions or values. In effect, he becomes like Arrowsmith. As I said, Arrowsmith too has a certain integrity and determination in regard to his work, but the (totally unexplained) difference between his professional attitude and his behavior as a man is so vast that the character does not integrate.

To understand a personality is like peeling off one onion skin after another. First you understand the immediate motive behind his actions. Then you ask: Why this motive? You peel off another skin and go into deeper motivation—until you come to grasp the fundamentals of the personality. The same applies to characterization in fiction.

To allow Roark such a line as "I'm not always sure, but I am about my work" is to say that he has integrity professionally, but not otherwise. That is a one-layer, one-onion-skin explanation: for some unstated reason, Roark has integrity in regard to architecture. But left open are the wider questions: Why in regard to architecture? and: Why not in regard to other matters?

This brings us to the difference between Naturalism and Romanticism in characterization. The Naturalistic method is to present only *one* layer of motivation; the Romantic method is to look not only at the immediate onion skin, but as deep as the author can go.

The Naturalist presents merely the immediate reason for a character's actions; for instance, if a man is unscrupulous about money, it is because he is "greedy." The Romanticist goes deeper and indicates *why* a man is greedy, and perhaps even what is the nature of greed.

In *The Fountainhead*, I show that Roark is motivated by his love for the profession of architecture—but I do not stop there. I go deeper: What is the meaning of a love for a creative profession? And deeper: What does such love rest on? It rests on an independent mind. And deeper: What is the moral meaning of an independent mind?

Similarly, I show that Peter Keating wants prestige, money, and conventional success, but I also go several onion skins deeper. I ask: Why does a man go after money and prestige? Why is Peter Keating so anxious for popular approval? I show that a second-hander has no independent judgment and can derive his self-esteem only from the approval of others. And I go deeper: Why does a man decide to depend on the judgment of others? Ultimately, because of his refusal to think for himself.

I show Roark's motives and the motives of his enemies; and I show why the two have to clash. Starting from the first layer of the action—the struggle of an architect—I go all the way down to the fundamental, metaphysical issue: the independent mind versus the second-hand mind.

The characterizations in *The Fountainhead* can be read on as many levels as the reader's understanding permits. If he is interested only in the immediate motivation and meaning of actions, he can see that Roark is motivated by art and Keating by money. But if he wants to see more, he can also see the meaning of these choices and, deeper, what in human nature is at their root.

In *Arrowsmith*, by contrast, we learn that Arrowsmith is motivated by love for pure science—period. We learn nothing deeper about his motivation. The same applies to some of his fellow college students, who are motivated differently, by love for money or the desire for an easy practice. All this *is* motivation; and within the limits of these motives, the characters are well drawn. For instance, the character Angus Duer is the Peter Keating of the story—the smart, unscrupulous young man who is after money and prestige through manipulating people. He is presented clearly and consistently. The author *does* indicate what moves him. But he indicates merely the first onion skin.

If you are a perceptive but superficial observer and you look at people in real life, you can deduce one or two layers of motivation behind their actions. This is all that Lewis presents. By a "superficial" observer, I do not mean a stupid one (Lewis is by no means stupid). I mean "nonphilosophical." I mean someone who does not think too abstractly about the nature of man or of human motivation.

In Romantic characterization, the reader is given as much human psychology as a writer's ambition and ability permit. In Naturalistic characterization, by contrast, great physical detail is given about moving figures without any real psychology.

Observe what Tolstoy does in *Anna Karenina*. The central conflict is that a woman of stronger life energy leaves her mediocre husband to elope with a young officer. We never learn anything about the psychology of the characters. All we learn is that Anna Karenina has a desire for happiness and is impatient with her conventional husband; that her husband has a helpless, grasping desire to hold her; and that the young lover is sort of dashing and is really in love.

What is the meaning of a woman's desire for happiness? Does a husband have the right to hold his wife by sheer convention, and what would *that* mean? If a young officer in nineteenth-century Russia (which was more mid-Victorian than any other European country) would ruin his career in order to elope with a married woman, what would make him do it?

"Sexual passion." The book gives answers like that.

The subtler details of the psychological relationships, such as who says what at which moment, are very skillfully presented; Tolstoy's characterizations are full of the kind of minute details one would observe if one watched a family tragedy through a transparent wall. But such details merely give one the first layer of motivation in the persons involved—which is all that Tolstoy presents. The deeper meaning of the motives is never given.

This is why I say that Naturalistic characters have no human psychology. They are human beings who have certain motives—and that's that. The author goes no deeper than their immediately available motivation, nor do the characters themselves ever question their own souls or the deeper meaning behind their souls.

The reason why a Naturalist approaches characterization this way is his basic philosophical determinism. If one views man as a determined being, one necessarily does not go deeply into what makes him move. He is what he is. If he acts in a certain way, one says: "Well, then he has *this* kind of passion." What makes a mind center on such a passion? A Naturalist does not ask this question; it is not relevant to his view of man. He takes men ready-made.

A Naturalist tells you that men act in a certain way, but not *why* they do so; or (if he is a serious Naturalist) he gives some indication, but a comparatively superficial one. He always stops short of any fundamental "Why?"—of any issue pertaining to *all* human beings. He never touches the *universals* of human behavior, because to do so would be contrary to the premise that men are determined. There is no place in the philosophy of determinism for wide, universal abstractions that govern human behavior and among which men have the power to choose.

The Romantic method, by contrast, goes down to fundamental abstractions. This is not to say that *every* Romanticist does so; but every Romanticist goes as deep as his personal ambition or his subject requires. The *essence* of the Romantic method is to present the universals motivating human action.

This is true even of Romantic literature that is not too serious. For instance, take Victor Hugo, who is not a serious student of human nature, but more the Romantic dramatist—and take *Notre-Dame de Paris*, which is the nearest parallel to *Anna Karenina*. Being the story of a priest's love for a Gypsy girl, it also has the conflict of guilty passion as a general theme.

Even though Hugo does not give a detailed study of the priest's psychology, he presents the *essentials* of the conflict of a man torn between a great religious devotion and a guilty bodily passion for a beautiful woman. By means of his story, he presents not merely the conflict of *this* priest with *this* dancer, but the whole soul-body issue, including the meaning of such a conflict; and his characterizations, while not too perceptive, are built on a level consonant with such a purpose.

Hugo presents the abstraction behind the particular conflict of the priest in a way that Tolstoy would never dream of doing. Being on the free-will premise, Hugo knows that a man's actions are motivated by his choices, and that his choices go deeper than the immediate impulse of the moment. It is not an accident that this man is a priest. Why is he a priest? What basic view of life has made him devote his life to religion? And what conflict in that devotion has made him capable of betraying his religion? Hugo makes characterization an issue of free will all the way down to the roots of a human personality.

Tolstoy, by contrast, spends volumes detailing every movement and emotion and shading of voice of a woman torn between her duty to her husband and her love for another man—and we learn nothing about what in a human psychology would put a woman in such a position. We learn only that this woman happened to be caught in it because "she wanted to live." Why did she want to live? One does not ask "Why?" Men are what they are.

Characters who represent moral or philosophical issues are usually called "archetypes." I object to that word in this context, because an "archetype" is supposed to be a walking abstraction without individuality. The art (and difficulty) of Romantic characterization is to present the archetypical—that which is typical of any individualist like Roark or any second-hander like Keating—while at the same time giving enough specific detail so that the character comes across as *this* particular human being.

People refer to Romantic characterizations as "archetypes" not because the individuality is lacking, but because the abstraction shows, and shows by the author's intention. The particular details of a personality are given, but they are never accidental or irrelevant; they are related to the wider abstraction and deeper motivation of the type of man presented.

Any reader can tell that *The Fountainhead* is a book not only about an architect from the 1920s to 1940s, but about any innovator in any period or profession. Why? Because I cover the essence of all the issues involved, starting with the most basic issue: the independent mind versus the second-hand mind. Everything I present relating to the conflict of Roark and Keating can be translated (changing only the professional details) into the struggle between any men representing these human attitudes in any profession at any time.

I present characters—in *The Fountainhead* and in everything else I have written—by means of that which is *essential* to men on certain kinds of premises.

Contrast this to the characterization of Arrowsmith, which contains a great deal that is totally accidental. Arrowsmith's devotion to medicine can, as an abstraction, pertain to other doctors, or to any idealist in any profession. But his feelings toward his fraternity, his troubles in deciding what job to take, his hesitations in regard to women—these do not pertain to the issues of "ambitious doctor" or "struggling idealist," or to anything else of a thematic nature. They are accidental details of the kind that might be present in any personality, but that have no wider significance.

This is the essence of a Naturalist's approach to characterization. He presents a character whose universality—i.e., application to other men—is only statistical. For instance, he presents a typical Midwestern young man of a certain period, or a typical ambitious doctor. Then he gives that character accidental traits within the range of the statistical assignment. If these traits are consistent with the particular statistical type, the result is a good contemporary characterization. The reader feels: "Yes, I've seen that type of man." But what comes across from the jumble of accidental details is merely the character's immediate motivation, plus his temporal and geographical averageness.

Arrowsmith is an extremely intelligent presentation of the atmosphere of medical schools and medical careers of a certain period. When I first read it [in the 1920s], it seemed quite interesting, in the sense that an intelligent newspaper article about contemporary personalities is interesting. Today, *Arrowsmith* is like last year's newspaper.

If one were to ask, "How does this story apply to any other profession than medicine, or to medicine in any other period than the one presented?" one could give only the most generalized answer. One could say: "In essence, every idealist, every man of integrity, will face a struggle." That is all. Beyond the general conception of an idealist's struggle, everything in the book is devoted to the minute details of Arrowsmith's profession and period.

There are two ways in which people can regard characters in fiction and recognize them. For instance, one often hears that character X is "just like the folks next door." This is the slogan of the Naturalistic school: its characters are "like the folks next door." The people who consider such characters "real" are usually those who do not consider abstract characters real. They are the ones who tell me that I write about men who do not exist.

On the other hand, people who *can* think in terms of essentials tell me that I write about the kind of men they see all over the place. A number of people have told me the names of architects I never heard of, swearing that I copied Peter Keating from them. You can see why. Since I present the essence of that which creates a second-hander like Keating, they can recognize in him many men who do not have his particular appearance, mannerisms, or personal problems, but who have the same essence.

Now compare the following two scenes from *Arrowsmith* and *The Fountainhead*. In both, the author's assignment is to present the relationship of the novel's hero—a young student who will later become a brilliant scientist (Arrowsmith) or architect (Roark)—to the particular teacher whom he has selected and from whom he will get the proper training.

Read first the scene from *Arrowsmith*, which portrays Arrowsmith's initial meeting with Max Gottlieb, the most brilliant and most unpopular professor at his school.

> "Vell? Yes?"
>
> "Oh, Professor Gottlieb, my name is Arrowsmith. I'm a medic freshman, Winnemac B.A. I'd like awfully to take bacteriology this fall instead of next year. I've had a lot of chemistry—"
>
> "No. It is not time for you."
>
> "Honest, I know I could do it now."
>
> "There are two kinds of students the gods give me. One kind they

dump on me like a bushel of potatoes. I do not like potatoes, and the potatoes they do not ever seem to have great affection for me, but I take them and teach them to kill patients. The other kind—they are very few!—they seem for some reason that is not at all clear to me to wish a liddle bit to become scientists, to work with bugs and make mistakes. Those, ah, those, I seize them, I denounce them, I teach them right away the ultimate lesson of science, which is to wait and doubt. Of the potatoes, I demand nothing; of the foolish ones like you, who think I could teach them something, I demand everything. No. You are too young. Come back next year."

"But honestly, with my chemistry—"

"Have you taken physical chemistry?"

"No, sir, but I did pretty well in organic."

"Organic chemistry! Puzzle chemistry! Stink chemistry! Drugstore chemistry! Physical chemistry is power, it is exactness, it is life. But organic chemistry—that is a trade for potwashers. No. You are too young. Come back in a year."

Now read the scene from *The Fountainhead*, which portrays Roark's initial meeting with Henry Cameron.

"Well?" said Cameron at last. "Did you come to see me or did you come to look at pictures?"

Roark turned to him.

"Both," said Roark.

He walked to the desk. People had always lost their sense of existence in Roark's presence; but Cameron felt suddenly that he had never been as real as in the awareness of the eyes now looking at him.

"What do you want?" snapped Cameron.

"I should like to work for you," said Roark quietly. The voice said: "I should like to work for you." The tone of the voice said: "I'm going to work for you."

"Are you?" said Cameron, not realizing that he answered the unpronounced sentence. "What's the matter? None of the bigger and better fellows will have you?"

"I have not applied to anyone else."

"Why not? Do you think this is the easiest place to begin? Think anybody can walk in here without trouble? Do you know who I am?"

"Yes. That's why I'm here."

"Who sent you?"

"No one."

"Why the hell should you pick me?"

"I think you know that."

Roark then shows his drawings to Cameron. Now read the conclusion of the scene:

"God damn you," said Cameron softly.

"God damn you!" roared Cameron suddenly, leaning forward. "I didn't ask you to come here! I don't need any draftsmen! There's nothing here to draft! I don't have enough work to keep myself and my men out of the Bowery Mission! I don't want any fool visionaries starving around here! I don't want the responsibility. I didn't ask for it. I never thought I'd see it again. I'm through with it. I was through with that many years ago. I'm perfectly happy with the drooling dolts I've got here, who never had anything and never will have and it makes no difference what becomes of them. That's all I want. Why did you have to come here? You're setting out to ruin yourself, you know that, don't you? And I'll help you to do it. I don't want to see you. I don't like you. I don't like your face. You look like an insufferable egotist. You're impertinent. You're too sure of yourself. Twenty years ago I'd have punched your face with the greatest of pleasure. You're coming to work here tomorrow at nine o'clock sharp."

"Yes," said Roark, rising.

"Fifteen dollars a week. That's all I can pay you."

"Yes."

"You're a damn fool. You should have gone to someone else. I'll kill you if you go to anyone else. What's your name?"

"Howard Roark."

"If you're late, I'll fire you."

"Yes."

Roark extended his hand for the drawings.

"Leave these here!" bellowed Cameron. "Now get out!"

In this scene, Cameron is speaking about a concrete—his own and Roark's particular position in the world—but at the same time he is stating and emphasizing a wider issue—their stand against society as individualists and nonconformists. Cameron is saying: "We're outcasts, we'll have a terrible battle, I don't want you to suffer as I did—but you have no choice, because I won't let you sell yourself by going to anyone else." This is the essence of the bond between the two men and the key to their fate in the book.

Compare this to the scene from *Arrowsmith*. Gottlieb too is a nonconformist and a lonely, idealistic fighter, although this is indicated more in the preceding narrative than in the scene itself. What *is* projected in the scene is Gottlieb's contempt for the average students ("the potatoes") and his eagerness to find serious disciples (those who wish "to become scientists"). In other words, he feels strongly about his science and is bitterly opposed to the conventional standards. However, since he is talking in concretes which illustrate merely that one level of abstraction, his speech has a nonphilosophical aura. He likes one type of student and is bitter about the other—period.

Cameron says openly that he and Roark are victims of society and fighters for their art; Gottlieb says nothing that indicates his wider position as a fighter for science. Instead, he focuses on the minutiae of his particular profession, such as the requirements for his course or the issue of organic versus physical chemistry. From a Naturalistic standpoint, these technical details are what makes the scene "real"; from a Romantic standpoint, they clutter it up. Observe that I do not have Cameron say: "I'll teach you to design corner windows rather than Greek pediments." But the Naturalist's approach is precisely the inclusion of such details. "To be real," he would say, "you've got to give the particulars."

If the scene from *Arrowsmith* had been longer and fuller, and if it had shown the essence of the two men's encounter, it could, even by the Romantic standard, have absorbed some of the technical details. The number of concrete details proper to include in a scene depends on its scale. But as the scene stands, one can only infer the essence, since what is shown directly is merely the technical dialogue. This is why I say that the scene is cluttered with details.

Whether a writer draws a character in essentials or in minute detail is determined by the depth of motivation he covers.

A Romantic characterization must not include too many particulars; it can include only that which is essential to each layer of the onion skins—of the character's motives.

For instance, the characterization of Cameron in *The Fountainhead* is very generalized. The reader is not told much about his life, his office, or his clothes. But what *do* I show about him? Not merely that he is a great man who is misunderstood by society and then drinks himself to death—but also the reasons behind it. Cameron is an independent man who has been broken by [an inimical] society; he is a man who could have been like Roark, but his premises and confidence were not strong enough. I bring everything I say about him down to the basic issue: a man's mind against the minds of others.

All I present is the essentials. Therefore, while Cameron *is* Cameron, he also stands for any great man who, after a devoted struggle, is broken by society.

Gottlieb is presented much more intimately by Lewis. For instance, he makes a special kind of delicate European sandwich for Arrowsmith, he uses expressions like "Father Nietzsche" and "Father Schopenhauer," and he refers to his days as a student in Heidelberg. This *is* good characterization; one does get the picture of the man, and in great detail—almost as if one had seen his photograph. But what does one learn about his motivation? Only one thing: that he is devoted to science and has contempt for worldly goods and human relationships.

Sinclair Lewis will beat me hollow on the perception of the particular. But the particular is all that the reader gets from him, with merely one or two underlying levels of motivation.

Incidentally, there are instances of crossbreeding in literature, Shakespeare being the best example. He presents his characters by means of their essence—the essence of a dominating father (King Lear), of a doubting intellectual (Hamlet), or of a jealous man (Othello). Yet Shakespeare is a determinist, and a [precursor] of the Naturalistic school; he believes that man is a plaything of fate, carrying within himself some tragic flaw that ultimately destroys him. For instance, Othello is jealous, but it is never explained *why*; he is simply possessed by jealousy as other men are possessed by greed or love. It's in his nature, and he is helpless against it. Shakespeare presents human essences on the basis of the kind of determinist philosophy that most of mankind shares, which is one reason for his immortality. He is the grandest literary representative of that philosophy.

The critics who complain that Romantic characters are oversimplified "archetypes"—"just heroes and villains"—would say about the Roark-Cameron scene that it portrays merely "gruff old professor" and "idealistic student." But it is actually the Arrowsmith-Gottlieb scene that portrays such stock characters.

Roark and Cameron are abstractions of profound issues—and the concretes which are shown indicate those issues. By contrast, Lewis presents many more details, but they do not add up to any consistent depth. The result is precisely a wooden archetype like "gruff old professor"—because nobody can retain all the tiny, insignificant details. They vanish from the reader's mind, and the abstraction that remains represents merely the first onion skin of motivation. The characters are overdetailed and never fully real.

Now observe that nobody would *normally* speak the way Cameron does, nor would a professor in Gottlieb's position normally speak as *he* does merely because he saw something promising in a student. What, then, would make an admirer of Naturalism consider Gottlieb realistic, as opposed to Cameron? The touch of the ludicrous.

When Gottlieb says, "I do not like potatoes, and the potatoes they do not ever seem to have great affection for me, but I take them and teach them to kill patients," his idea is simply: "They send me too many mediocrities. I don't like mediocrities." But his use of a homey, undignified metaphor—"potatoes"—gives him a touch of the ludicrous, the vulgar, the nonheroic. He is made "human"; he is given verbal feet of clay. That is what would make a reader on the Naturalist premise say: "Yes, he's real. People do talk that way."

In fact, they do *not* talk that way. Further, Gottlieb is not supposed to be an average man; he is supposed to be a man of genius. But to a Naturalist, a man cannot be an exception; he has to be a statistical average. Just as, according to the saying, no man can be a hero to his valet, so, according to Naturalism, no character can be a hero to his author. In Naturalistic literature, therefore, if a man is presented as great, he will always have a tragic flaw, a human infirmity, feet of clay. There will always be an undercutting touch—and no undercutting is more deadly, artistically, than humor. Nothing is better calculated to make a great man appear ludicrous than a touch of humor at the wrong time.

On the other side, what a Naturalist would object to in Cameron's speech is not anything Cameron specifically says, but the fact that his speech is direct, undiluted, purposeful. It is not a method of Naturalism to focus anything sharply.

Let us now ask: Is Arrowsmith a realistic character and Roark an unrealistic one?

Both of the above scenes present a young man with a serious purpose, starting out on a serious career, and I would say that Arrowsmith is ten times more unrealistic and unnatural than Roark. He says: "I'd like awfully to take bacteriology this fall instead of next year," and "Honest, I know I could do it now." I submit that no serious, dedicated young man ever talks that way.

An intelligent young man with a purpose is, in his late teens and early twenties, particularly solemn and formal. He might be shy and unable to express himself fully, but then, the shyer and more uncertain he is, the more formal he will be. If such a young man approaches someone he admires in his profession, he does not come across like a college football player, saying: "Oh, gee, honest." Had Lewis genuinely been watching reality, he would have presented Arrowsmith in any way but this.

Arrowsmith's stammering embarrassment and nonserious enthusiasm reflects the atmosphere of collegiate dialogue of his period. It represents Lewis's statistical abstraction of an average college kid; it does not represent anyone's realistic picture of a serious young man approaching a professor he reveres.

Now consider Roark. He comes to the man he worships and calmly says, "I should like to work for you," implying: "I'm going to work for you." No young man, a Naturalist would object, could be that poised and self-assured. My answer is: That depends on what *kind* of young man one is talking about and what premises he has set himself.

When I say that no serious young man would act like Arrowsmith, am I going by the statistical method? No; I am going by logic. It is in the nature of a serious young mind not to be casual about its concerns.

But if I were to follow the Naturalistic method of studying real people, I would submit as an example Leonard Peikoff, whom I met when he was seventeen and who was very much afraid of meeting me—afraid in the sense of "awed." He had a long list of philosophical questions he wanted me to answer, but when he came to my house, he asked his companions if they would please go in and let him stay in the car. (I learned this only years later.) When he did come in, he was obviously ill at ease, in the sense not of foolishness, but of tension. So I asked him: "How did you like the drive?"—trying to do a little small talk to help him relax. And it was he, at seventeen, who said: "Well, let's get down to business."

That is what I would present if I were a Naturalist—only then it would be Romanticism.

Like everything else in writing, a characterization cannot be created by conscious calculation.

Take the Roark-Keating scene. Suppose you made a list of Roark's virtues—independent, rational, just, honest—and decided to consult that list each time you came to a line of dialogue. You would not be able to make Roark utter a single line. Nothing would occur to you; and even if something did, you would have to spend a month figuring out: "If Roark says, 'Why not?' does that conform to the list? Or if he says, 'Oh well, I didn't mind it,' does that conform?"

In other words, you cannot figure out consciously the kind of implications I explained when I compared the two Roark-Keating scenes—and I mentioned only the crucial points of difference between the scenes. I could spend two full lectures explaining the implications of and motivations behind the lines in those two scenes alone. It is as complex as that.

You cannot create a character from philosophical abstractions alone; you cannot approach characterization merely by telling yourself: "My hero will be independent, just, rational." The process is indirect—you must know how to use your subconscious. You must know how consciously to prepare it so that it will make the right selections for you.

Your characterizations will never be better than your power of observation. A human mind does not first conceive of floating abstractions and then, by means of them, recognize the concretes; in order properly to grasp an abstraction, you must *derive* it from concretes. To prepare your subconscious for writing proper characterization, therefore, you must be a good observer and introspector.

You constantly react to people—you approve or disapprove, like or dislike, are encouraged or uneasy. You estimate emotionally everyone you meet. Learn to introspect in the sense of accounting for what in a person causes your reaction. Do not go through life saying: "I don't like X. Why? How do I know? I just don't like him." That will never make you a writer. Instead, if you feel a strong dislike for someone, then, as your artistic assignment, identify *what* you dislike, and by what means you observed it.

For instance, a man is rude to you, and you do not like it. What in particular is rude? Is it the implication of what the man says? Is it his voice or manner? Why do you dislike it? File this in your subconscious. Another time, you meet a man who is charming. Do not merely say: "I don't know why, but I like this man. He's wonderful." Identify: What is charming about him? How does he convey it? How did you observe it? File this away. By being a constant, conscious valuer of people, you gather the material from which you will draw your future characterizations.

If you have learned a great many abstractions that you have not yet connected to concretes, do the reverse. For instance, if you decide that you favor independence, observe which words or gestures or manners of people convey independence to you. And, conversely, observe what conveys dependence. What conveys honesty? What conveys dishonesty? You can observe these characteristics only by their outward manifestations—by the words, actions, gestures, and subtler mannerisms of people.

When your subconscious is stocked with such well-filed material—when your concretes are filed under the proper abstractions and your abstractions are amply illustrated by concretes—then you can approach an assignment such as "present a characterization of Roark." And then, if you tell yourself that he is independent, honest, and just, your subconscious will throw at you the kind of concretes that make you feel, while writing a scene: "Yes, Roark would say this, but he would not say that."

The best, most natural dialogue is usually written as if the writer is listening to dictation. You might get stuck on any particular point and have to question yourself; but normally, dialogue writes itself. You have an idea of the scene, and when you write, the dialogue "just comes" to you—exactly as, in a conversation, your own answers come to you. That is, you speak from your premises, knowledge, and estimate of the situation.

In writing dialogue, you must react on two or more premises. As Roark, you speak from a certain premise; as Keating, you say something else. Your mind must know the connection between certain abstractions and their concrete expressions so well that you can write for three or five or any number of people, constantly switching premises in your mind. You cannot do this by conscious intention. You must reach the stage where the process feels "instinctive"—where, the moment when you speak for Roark, you have a sense of what he would say, and when Keating has to answer, you have a sense of what *he* would say.

This sudden "feel" of a character is not a mystical talent. In the process of writing, you feel that you "just know" what Roark or Keating would say; but this feeling means only that your understanding of the premises involved has become automatic.

When I wrote the Roark-Keating scene, I did not think consciously of those implications of each line that I explained earlier. But when I write a line inspirationally, I *can* tell myself why it is in character, and why another line would be out of character. To judge the objective validity of what you write, you must be able *afterward* to tell yourself why a given line is right for one character (what it conveys) and why something else is right for another character (what *it* conveys). After the writing, you must be able to do the kind of analysis I did of the Roark-Keating scene.

At first you should do this kind of analysis every time you write something, in order to train yourself in the process. Later, all your rational justifications will be in order and available to your conscious mind, but you will not have to check on them each time. You will know by a lightning-like sum what kind of touch is right, and why it is right.

Also, when you begin writing, *write only as much as you are sure of.* Do not force your characters into artificial behavior; do not say arbitrarily: "I don't know what he'd say, so I'll put in the first line available." If you do not know what a character would do or say, you simply have to give it some more thought.

When I create a character, I find it helpful to project him visually. This gives me a concrete focus so that the character does not float in my mind as a mere collection of abstract virtues or vices. Seeing his appearance is like having a physical body on which I can hang the abstractions.

That is how Roark was created. I did not base him on any particular human being; but the start of the character in my mind was the image of a redheaded man with long legs and gaunt cheekbones. I formed as clear an image of his figure as I could, and this became the focus for all the abstract characteristics I had to give him. I have done the same for all of my heroes.

In regard to villains and characters who are neither particularly good nor bad, I find it helpful to focus on some acquaintance or public figure—not on the details of this person, but only on the essence. In the case of Toohey, I had in mind four living journalists and writers. I did not think of any one of them in specific detail, nor did I study their writings or lives. But my total impression of them gave me valuable clues to the manifestations of certain basic premises. These figures were the concretes that helped me to hold it all in my mind. This was the preliminary gathering of material.

Then, one day, some acquaintances invited me to a lecture by a liberal at the New School for Social Research. I felt that it would be immoral to go; but they insisted that the lecturer was not leftist, that he was a brilliant speaker, and that they had already bought the tickets, so I went. And there was Toohey in the flesh, in personal appearance and manner. [The speaker was the British Labour Party politician Harold Laski.]

When he spoke, that man projected infinitely more than the

specific content of his ideas. It is true that he was not particularly liberal—that is, he was the most vicious liberal I have ever heard in public, but not blatantly so. He was very subtle and gracious, he rambled on a great deal about nothing in particular—and then he made crucial, vicious points once in a while. My foolish acquaintances did not know what was going on, but I did, and I thought: "*There* is my character."

I did not read anything about him; I did not care to know much. But what I gained from his appearance and way of speaking was the lightning-like sum of the kind of personality that certain premises would produce. Anytime I would ask myself, for instance, how Toohey would act toward his niece, or what his attitude would be toward young love, I had only to remember the image of that man on the speaker's pulpit and I would know unerringly what his type would do.

I was using an abstraction, not a concrete. I was not copying a real-life model; from a political lecture, I had no way of knowing what the speaker's attitude would be toward a niece or young love. He served merely to concretize and anchor certain abstractions in my mind.

Years later, I learned that the speaker's career was in fact somewhat like Toohey's: he was always the man behind the scenes, much more influential than anybody knew publicly, pulling the strings behind the governments of several countries. Finally he was proved to be a communist, which he did not announce himself as or blatantly sound like. This demonstrates my "writer's instinct." I observed the total impression of the man, I derived my own concretes, and in many instances they were similar to the facts—proving not that I was clairvoyant, but that I had grasped the right abstractions and translated them correctly.

This is the method I recommend (but if it seems too cumbersome, do not treat it as a duty). You do not literally copy a person; you use him as a concretization of something too complex to hold in your mind as a mere philosophical or literary description.

The result is that you have a sense of what your character would do or say without having to figure it all out in advance. You have caught the basic tone, the key, of a personality.

8

Style I: Depictions of Love

When I was writing *Atlas Shrugged*, I spent a long time planning the scene where Francisco comes to Dagny in the country. Many issues had to be integrated in this very complex scene, and I was exhausted after days of walking and thinking on the road in front of my house in California. One day I told [my husband] Frank that I was tired of planning the scene. He knew about its content, and, not too seriously, he told me: "Oh, that's simple. All you have to say is: 'He rushes up the hill, he seizes her in his arms, he kisses her—and she likes it.' "

Everything between that sentence and what you read in *Atlas Shrugged* comes under the department of *style*.

The swiftness of Francisco's movements was carrying him toward the hill while he was raising his head to glance up. He saw her above, at the door of the cabin, and stopped. She could not distinguish the expression on his face. He stood still for a long moment, his face raised to her. Then he started up the hill.

She felt—almost as if she had expected it—that this was a scene from their childhood. He was coming toward her, not running, but moving upward with a kind of triumphant, confident eagerness. No, she thought, this was not their childhood—it was the future as she would have seen it then, in the days when she waited for him as for her release from prison. It was a moment's view of a morning they would have reached, if her vision of life had been fulfilled, if they had both gone the way she had then been so certain of going. Held motionless by wonder, she stood looking at him, taking this moment, not in the name of the present, but as a salute to their past.

When he was close enough and she could distinguish his face, she saw the look of that luminous gaiety which transcends the solemn by proclaiming the great innocence of a man who has earned the right to be light-hearted. He was smiling and whistling some piece of music that seemed to flow like the long, smooth, rising flight of his steps. The melody seemed distantly familiar to her, she felt that it belonged with this moment, yet she felt also that there was something odd about it, something important to grasp, only she could not think of it now.

"Hi, Slug!"

"Hi, Frisco!"

She knew—by the way he looked at her, by an instant's drop of his eyelids closing his eyes, by the brief pull of his head striving to lean back and resist, by the faint, half-smiling, half-helpless relaxation of his lips, then by the sudden harshness of his arms as he seized her—that it was involuntary, that he had not intended it, and that it was irresistibly right for both of them.

The desperate violence of the way he held her, the hurting pressure of his mouth on hers, the exultant surrender of his body to the touch of hers, were not the form of a moment's pleasure—she knew that no physical hunger could bring a man to this—she knew that it was the statement she had never heard from him, the greatest confession of love a man could make. No matter what he had done to wreck his life, this was still the Francisco d'Anconia in whose bed she had been so proud of belonging—no matter what betrayals she had met from the world, her vision of life had been true and some indestructible part of it had remained within him—and in answer to it, her body responded to his, her arms and mouth held him, confessing her desire, confessing an acknowledgment she had always given him and always would.

In effect, what takes place in the scene is exactly what Frank said. The difference between his sentence and the final execution depends on the style.

That which can be synopsized in a brief sentence—theme, plot, characterization—is the "what" of a novel or play. Style is the "how"—it is that which cannot be synopsized.

You have probably heard that some story "isn't much, but it's the way it's done." This remark is warranted when the plot or message is slight, but the style good.

I divide the issue of style into two broad categories: the selection of content and the selection of words.

The "selection of content" is those aspects of an assignment that a writer chooses to communicate. For instance, in describing a room, one writer might give a minute catalogue of its every object. Another writer might select the essentials, that which gives the room its character. A third writer might say something neither exhaustive nor essential, but inconclusive, such as: "It was a narrow room with pale walls and some chairs."

In the Dagny-Francisco scene, *what* I really had to present was Frank's synopsis sentence. But what kind of elements would I include in order to describe how Francisco rushes up the hill, or how he seizes Dagny in his arms, or what she feels? Would I describe the scenery? include dialogue? narrate their thoughts? That is selection of content.

The "selection of words" is what is commonly understood by "style": a writer's choice of words and method of constructing sentences. Here you will see, as we study examples, the most startling variations. As with fingerprints, there are as many possible styles as there are men. No matter what the number of people who share the same philosophy, no one need ever be imitative of another's style. In the selection and order of words, so many possibilities exist that you never have to worry about whether you will achieve an individual style. You will achieve it; but only if you do *not* aim at it consciously.

Style is the most complex of the elements of writing, and must be left to "instinct." I have explained why even plot and characterization cannot be created fully by conscious calculation, but depend on subconscious, automatized premises. This is even more true of style.

In style, form follows function. In other words, what determines your style is your purpose—both in the book as a whole and in each paragraph or sentence. But given the number of issues involved in even the simplest story, there is no way to calculate the function and form consciously. Therefore, you have to set your literary premises and then write without self-consciousness. Write as it comes to you, on such premises as you have.

Do not decide to have a "brusque" style, a "dramatic" style, a "sensitive" style, or whatever nonsense you might have heard in literary schools. No such lines can be drawn. Above all, never imitate anyone else's style. Some writing schools ask students to write a story in the style of Sinclair Lewis, and another one in the style of Thomas Mann, and another one in the stream-of-consciousness style. Nothing could be deadlier: this is a sure way never to acquire a style of your own. A style comes from the combination of all of a writer's purposes and premises (and not only his literary ones). You cannot borrow another man's soul, and you cannot borrow his style. You would only be a cheap imitator.

Write as purposefully and clearly as you can, on your own premises, and your style will develop with practice. If you have set yourself some literary premises, the elements of your future style will be apparent in your first attempts. But it is impossible for anyone to have a recognizable style of his own prior to practicing. Given the complexity involved, a style has to become automatic before it can be thoroughly individual and polished.

If, after some years of work, you feel that your way of expression is not right, you have to do more thinking about what you do and do not like in literature. Identify what your style is missing, what category the error belongs to; then identify the right premise, which will enable you to express things more exactly or colorfully.

But never try to force a style. When someone is writing in a phony manner, it is as apparent as a neon sign. It is much better, even if your writing is slightly awkward, to be natural.

I have selected some passages which I consider stylistically typical. They fall into three groups: the first six quotations deal with the subject of love, the next two are descriptions of nature, and the last four are descriptions of New York City. By seeing different writers treat the same subjects, you will be able to better identify their stylistic differences.

Look for what is accomplished in each quotation, and for the means by which it is accomplished. Identify first the "what"—the author's assignment; and then the "how"—the selection of content and of words.

In the first six quotations, as I said, the author's assignment is to present love, particularly the *intensity* of love.

From *Atlas Shrugged* by Ayn Rand

[The woman in these two different passages is Dagny Taggart, the man is John Galt. The "temple" is a powerhouse containing a motor which runs on atmospheric electricity and which has been invented by Galt.]

She was suddenly aware that they were alone; it was an awareness that stressed the fact, permitting no further implication, yet holding the full meaning of the unnamed in that special stress. They were alone in a silent forest, at the foot of a structure that looked like an ancient temple—and she knew what rite was the proper form of worship to be offered on an altar of that kind. She felt a sudden pressure at the base of her throat, her head leaned back a little, no more than to feel the faint shift of a current against her hair, but it was as if she were lying back in space, against the wind, conscious of nothing but his legs and the shape of his mouth. He stood watching her, his face still but for the faint movement of his eyelids drawing narrow as if against too strong a light. It was like the beat of three instants—this was the first—and in the next, she felt a stab of ferocious triumph at the knowledge that his effort and his struggle were harder to endure than hers—and then he moved his eyes and raised his head to look at the inscription on the temple. . . .

She collapsed, face down, on the bed. It was not the mere fact of physical exhaustion. It was the sudden monomania of a sensation too complete to endure. While the strength of her body was gone, while her mind had lost the faculty of consciousness, a single emotion drew on her remnants of energy, of understanding, of judgment, of control, leaving her nothing to resist it with or to direct it, making her unable to desire, only to feel, reducing her to a mere sensation—a static sensation without start or goal. She kept seeing his figure in her mind—his figure as he had stood at the door of the structure—she felt nothing else, no wish, no hope, no estimate of her feeling, no name for it, no relation to herself—there was no entity such as herself, she was not a person, only a function, the function of seeing him, and the sight was its own meaning and purpose, with no further end to reach.

My method here is to lead the reader to a certain abstraction—that this is a strong, violent love—by giving him a special kind of concretes. I select those touches of Dagny's experience that are *essential* to the nature of her feeling. How does the reader know that her feeling is not, say, a light infatuation? The concretes given do not pertain to infatuation.

To project the full reality of the scene, I present not merely what Dagny feels, but also that which she is responding to. Her emotion is not an introspective one; she feels it because she is looking at Galt in a certain place in a certain context. So I present, by means of essentials, a setting that creates a mood consonant with her emotion.

Possibly, a bird flew across the trees in this moment, or a butterfly fluttered somewhere. Dagny might even have been aware of these, on the edge of her consciousness. But to include them would have been disastrous. That would have been to follow the Naturalistic method of including accidental details; whereas I focus only on the essentials of Dagny's feeling and of the setting.

I always reproduce human awareness as it is experienced in reality, assuming a certain kind of character. (For instance, Dagny is not a woman who would be unaware of the exact nature of what she experiences. I showed *that* kind of psychology in the passages dealing with James Taggart.) In this moment, when Dagny is fully aware for the first time of her feeling for Galt, she would not think, "I'm madly in love," or "Love is an important value." One does not think like that. I project and reproduce that which *would* be the focus of Dagny's awareness.

The beginning of the first passage suggests Dagny's sudden physical awareness of Galt. "*She was suddenly aware that they were alone; it was an awareness that stressed the fact, permitting no further implication, yet holding the full meaning of the unnamed in that special stress. They were alone in a silent forest, at the foot of a structure that looked like an ancient temple—and she knew what rite was the proper form of worship to be offered on an altar of that kind.*" I suggest sex; it is a deliberate hint, without using the word. This passage follows a description of Galt's temple, which contains his invention; and I have planted earlier that Dagny regards sex as the expression of achievement and of one's highest values. The statement "*she knew what rite was the proper form of worship to be offered on an altar of that kind*" reminds the reader that the sight of a great achievement would lead Dagny to think of sex; my use of words like *temple*, *rite*, and *altar*, which connote religion or high values, reminds him that she considers sex a sacred value. The reader connects it all lightning-like in his mind: "Yes, she *would* feel that way, because of her attitude toward love and achievement."

The statement "*she knew what rite was the proper form of worship to be offered on an altar of that kind*" is literarily much stronger than, say, "she felt that she wanted to sleep with him." It is stronger because I make the *reader* draw the conclusion.

The next sentence brings the passage from the abstract down to the immediate moment, giving the sensory reality of Dagny's experience. Observe the slant: "*She felt a sudden pressure at the base of her throat*"—obviously a sexual emotion—"*her head leaned back a little, no more than to feel the faint shift of a current against her hair*"—a purely sensuous description—"*but it was as if she were lying back in space, against the wind*"—a deliberate stress on sexual connotations—"*conscious of nothing but his legs and the shape of his mouth.*" Had I said "conscious of nothing but him," it would have been too generalized (and not worth a cent). *What* is she conscious of? His legs and his mouth. These concretes emphasize her consciousness of one particular aspect of him, and thus one purpose. (In a more intellectual context, she would perhaps have been more conscious of his eyes.)

In the next sentence, I do the same in regard to him. "*He stood watching her, his face still but for the faint movement of his eyelids drawing narrow*"—first a physical description—"*as if against too strong a light.*" Since no strong light is involved in the scene, the implication is:

"against too strong a feeling." That is all I want to suggest; the context does the rest.

A difficult problem in emotional scenes is how to project that which, though made of different elements, would be experienced as one impact. In the next sentence, my technique is almost self-explanatory: "*It was like the beat of three instants—this was the first—and in the next, she felt a stab of ferocious triumph at the knowledge that his effort and his struggle were harder to endure than hers—and then he moved his eyes and raised his head to look at the inscription on the temple.*" Here I want the reader to think that he experienced the whole sentence as one. But he cannot experience it as one; I have to give the steps. So I start by unifying the steps into one whole—"*It was like the beat of three instants*"—and then I break it down into the three instants, which add up to the kind of progression that in real life *would* be experienced as one emotional impact.

In the second passage, I had one of the most difficult assignments: to present a violent emotion. The more violent an emotion, the less one is able to identify what it is made of. One just feels *it*, as a unity. "I feel something violent, and there are no words for it, and it can't be broken down into anything." I had to break the emotion down into the kind of concretes that Dagny would not really be thinking of, but that the reader would sum up into monomania.

I do it partly by means of negatives; I say what it is that Dagny does *not* have. "*A single emotion drew on her remnants of energy, of understanding, of judgment, of control*"—by concretizing the elements which are normally present in a consciousness, but which Dagny is now losing, I convey that hers is a violent emotion—"*leaving her nothing to resist it with or to direct it.*" I remind the reader that Dagny normally would not be at the mercy of a single emotion; but now she is.

Then I project that what she feels is love: "*She kept seeing his figure in her mind—his figure as he had stood at the door of the structure—she felt nothing else, no wish, no hope, no estimate of her feeling, no name for it, no relation to herself—there was no entity such as herself, she was not a person, only a function, the function of seeing him.*" To have said that she wanted to sleep with him, or that she realized she loved him, would have been weaker than saying that she is reduced to nothing but seeing his figure in her mind. Such conclusions as "I am in love with him" or "I want to marry him" are abstractions. They are *thoughts*, and would come later. The actual emotion would be experienced precisely as an extreme awareness of the other person, which is the essence of falling in love.

The conclusion conveys just that: "*and the sight was its own meaning and purpose, with no further end to reach.*" This is the extreme state of being in love, where the issue is not sex, or *any* purpose, but (to put it colloquially) only the awareness that the loved one exists—which then fills the whole world.

I make human epistemology my guide—in the selection of content and of words. I present the material as a human mind *would* perceive it in reality. All perception is selective. We are not cameras; in any given situation, no one sees everything. We see that which interests us, that which our values require us to focus on. When I write, I substitute *my* selectivity for the reader's; I present those highlights I want him to observe and leave him no room to focus on anything else. His awareness will then follow as if the material were actual reality. But he will be observing reality as *I* observe it—i.e., from my viewpoint, according to my value choice. (He can then decide what he thinks of these values, which is a different, private matter.)

My writing is both highly slanted and objective. It is slanted in that *I* select the focus; it is objective in that I do not *tell* the reader what to see or feel. I *show* it.

If I have an unimportant connecting sentence such as "They walked toward the car," that is telling, not showing—but then, by virtue of the matter's unimportance, there is nothing to show. Given the selectivity of human perception, this is how you do *in fact* experience a transition. If, in the middle of an important conversation, you are walking toward a car, you are aware, barely, of your direction; but that is not where your focus is. I use the same method to choose my content and my words.

I do not present the reader with anything but direct sensory evidence. The author, in my style, never speaks—yet the author is consciously pulling every string. I give the reader nothing but concrete, objective facts—slanted in such a way that he will have only the impression I intend him to have.

From *Notre-Dame de Paris* by Victor Hugo [translated by Ayn Rand]

From that day on, there was in me a man whom I did not know. I tried to use all my remedies, the cloister, the altar, the work, the books. Folly! Oh! science rings so hollow when one beats against it in despair a head full of passion! Do you know, young girl, what I always saw thenceforth between the book and me? You, your shadow, the image of the luminous apparition that had once moved across the space before me. But that image did not have the same color any longer; it was somber, ominous, dark like the black circle that pursues for a long time the sight of the reckless one who has looked fixedly at the sun.

Unable to get rid of it, always hearing your song humming in my head, always seeing your feet dancing on my prayer book, always feeling at night, in dreams, your shape slipping against my flesh, I wanted to see you again, to touch you, to know who you were, to see whether I would find you comparable to the ideal image I had kept of you, to shatter my dream perhaps by means of reality. In any case, I hoped that a new impression would efface the first, and the first had become unbearable to me. I sought you. I saw you again. Disaster! When I had seen you twice, I wished to see you a thousand times, I wished to see you always. Then—how can one stop on that steep descent into hell?—then I did not belong to myself any longer. The other end of the string that the devil had attached to my wings, he had tied it to your foot. I became a vagrant like you. I waited for you in doorways, I looked for you on street corners, I watched you from the top of my tower. Each evening, I returned to myself more charmed, more desperate, more bewitched, more lost! . . .

Oh, young girl, have pity on me! You believe that you are unhappy, alas! alas! you do not know what unhappiness is. Oh! to love a woman! to be a priest! to be hated! to love her with all the fury of one's soul, to feel that for the least of her smiles one would give one's blood, one's guts, one's character, one's salvation, immortality and eternity, this life and the next; to regret that one is not king, genius, emperor, archangel, God, that one might place a greater slave under her feet; to embrace her night and day with one's dreams and with

> one's thoughts; and to see her enamored of a soldier's uniform! and to have nothing to offer her but the squalid cassock of a priest that will arouse her fear and her disgust! . . . Do you know what it's like, that agony you are made to endure, through the long nights, by your arteries that boil, by your heart that bursts, by your head that splits, by your teeth that bite your hands; by these relentless tortures that keep turning you without respite, as upon a red-hot grid-iron, upon a thought of love, of jealousy and of despair! Young girl, mercy! relax for a moment! toss a few ashes on that flame! . . . Child! torture me with one hand, but caress me with the other! Have pity, young girl! have pity on me!

Hugo's assignment here is to convey the priest's intense passion and conflict. He conveys it by means of concretes—the priest does not merely say, "I suffered and I thought of you," he gives concretes—and the concretes are not irrelevant details; they underscore the essence of the priest's feelings. So Hugo and I have this in common: we deal in concretes and in essences.

For instance: *"I tried to use all my remedies, the cloister, the altar, the work, the books."* The priest does not say, "I tried to fight it," which would have been a generalization; he states the particular remedies he tried.

"Do you know, young girl, what I always saw thenceforth between the book and me? You, your shadow." This is a typically Romantic touch. Had he said, "I kept seeing your picture in my mind," that would not have been as strong as *"between the book and me."* One can almost *see* the girl dancing across a prayer book; the image is extremely colorful, and convincing, because it is specific. It gives one a sense of *how* he experienced his emotion—of how his concentration was broken by her image—which one would not get from a generality like "I constantly thought of you and nothing helped."

"Unable to get rid of it, always hearing your song humming in my head, always seeing your feet dancing on my prayer book"—again, concretizations which convey exactly what he experienced—*"always feeling at night, in dreams, your shape slipping against my flesh."* In one English-language edition, the translator says "seeing you in my dreams,"

which is a bromidic generalization and exactly the kind of sentence that Hugo would *not* write.

Observe the dramatic simplicity and concretization with which the priest gives his reasons for wanting to see the girl again: "*I wanted to see you again, to touch you, to know who you were, to see whether I would find you comparable to the ideal image I had kept of you, to shatter my dream perhaps by means of reality. . . . I sought you. I saw you again.*" Then he describes the consequences, and again he makes them concrete. He does not say: "From then on, I was helplessly committed to my passion." He says: "*I waited for you in doorways, I looked for you on street corners, I watched you from the top of my tower.*" Preceding this scene, a great deal has been established about the cathedral of Notre-Dame and its towers. The line "*I watched you from the top of my tower*" is thus an excellent concretization that evokes the whole context in the reader's mind: he can *see* the priest standing on the tower and the girl dancing in the square below.

"*Oh! to love a woman! to be a priest! to be hated!*" Strong concretes, naming the essence of the conflict. "*To feel that for the least of her smiles one would give one's blood, one's guts, one's character, one's salvation, immortality and eternity, this life and the next.*" Had he said, "I would give anything for your favor," it would have been a floating abstraction. "*And to see her enamored of a soldier's uniform!*"—not "of a stupid soldier," which would have been a weaker statement of the same idea—"*and to have nothing to offer her but the squalid cassock of a priest.*" By contrasting the garments, he projects the whole difference between the two lives: his own austere life versus the glamorous (in the girl's eyes) life of the soldier. This skillful use of two small concretes conveys the essence of the whole situation. "*Do you know what it's like, that agony you are made to endure, through the long nights, by your arteries that boil, by your heart that bursts, by your head that splits, by your teeth that bite your hands.*" He does not say: "I was tortured by the thought of you, night and day"; he gives particulars of how he experienced his torture—strong, startling particulars. The line "*by your teeth that bite your hands*" is a very good touch. The others are all exaggerations—arteries do not literally boil, a heart does not break, his head was not splitting—but one feels that he *did* bite his hands, and this conveys his agony very convincingly.

The line "*torture me with one hand, but caress me with the other!*" states the whole issue of the priest's conflict. It is an impossible thing to ask, but that is what makes it so dramatic an expression of his predicament: what he is asking of the girl *is* the impossible.

Although the priest does terrible things in the novel, one is never convinced that he is a total villain. Hugo obviously *intended* him as a villain, but, psychologically and philosophically, he was not sold on the idea. This conflict between Hugo's conscious convictions and his deepest, subconscious view of life shows in his style.

If Hugo's full conviction had been that the priest's passion is evil, the priest's way of speaking of his passion would have been much less attractive. He would have projected something ugly or sadistic—a perverted or evil feeling. But instead he speaks of his love in so romantic a way—the examples selected are so glowing and beautiful—that the reader necessarily feels sympathy for him (and so does the author).

In this passage, there are no exalted sentences in defense of religion. When the priest mentions religion, it is always in a blasphemous manner. In this particular projection, religion means nothing to him; he wants to put God under the girl's feet—which is wonderful, but not the way to project an evil passion.

If Hugo's own viewpoint had been what it ostensibly is—if he had really considered the priest a villain for his conflict—he would have presented the passion less attractively and religion more forcefully. But Hugo's subconscious is so much on the side of love and of this earth that I say: "May his God help him!"

Throughout the novel, the priest keeps announcing that his passion is "fate." In fact, earlier in his speech to the girl, he states that he lost the battle against temptation because God did not give to man a power as strong as the devil's. This is a deterministic premise. But what an author might have his characters say, or even what his own stated philosophy might be, is an issue totally different from what his actual, subconscious premises are—as this speech illustrates.

The speech expresses a violence of emotion that can come only from the possibility of *choice*. An automaton does not experience violent emotions. In literature written on the determinist premise, emotions of pain can be convincingly portrayed, but never a violent passion for a specific object on earth.

Observe the priest's self-assertion. He constantly tells how he tried to fight his passion; then, when he felt the desire to see the girl again, he watched and waited for her. He constantly talks about what he did; and he is begging her to have pity on him, by which he means: consent to love him. He is acting on his passion. He has decided that he cannot fight it any longer, so now he will try to win her. And his emotional violence has one purpose: "If I can convince her of the greatness of my love, then maybe I can win her." This is a man in charge of his own destiny.

If a man in a Naturalistic novel has a passion he cannot resist, there is an enormous tone of whining, amounting to: "Poor little me, I couldn't help it." Here, although the priest uses begging terms like *have pity on me* and *mercy*, his tone is not one of complaint.

I have already identified the method common to Hugo and me. Let me now point out certain differences between us.

First, Hugo permits more comment from the character himself—and thus from the author—than I would have done. For instance, the priest says: "*But that image did not have the same color any longer; it was somber, ominous, dark like the black circle that pursues for a long time the sight of the reckless one who has looked fixedly at the sun.*" A man talking of a passion might possibly use a metaphor. But here the priest is too literary: he turns an elegant phrase that Hugo himself might have written in narrative. This somewhat detracts from the reality of a man talking desperately and passionately.

Hugo is less concerned than I am with the exact (although slanted) re-creation of reality; he tends to interfere with his own presentation rather than stick to showing. This is more apparent in his narrative passages than in dialogue: in narrative, he often editorializes to the point of it being Hugo speaking. Incidentally, he comes across as the most fascinating speaker: the writing is brilliant; he always has something colorful to say. But he is nonobjective in permitting the presence of the author as a narrator.

Most nineteenth-century novelists did that. They editorialized constantly, even using expressions like "Now, gentle reader, we will let you in on a secret." This is a method of fiction writing which cannot be justified logically.

In the nineteenth century, writers were on the premise of writing as raconteurs, almost like the medieval troubadours who went around singing sagas. The author projected himself as a charming or witty personality—or an erudite one, like Hugo. But since the author *did* project himself, you have to read the novels of that time on two levels—which interrupts the reality. You are constantly taken out of the story itself, because you are listening to the narrator, and then you go back into the story.

This was merely a literary fashion, which was dropped—and ought to stay dropped. (Some people attempt to revive it, in a bad manner.) To remind the reader that somebody is telling him the story is to introduce an irrelevant element that destroys the attempt to re-create reality; it is as if a painter were to leave his brush in a corner of the canvas to remind you that he painted it. Fiction is an atheistic universe: you are the God who is creating it, but there must not be any God in your writing.

(If you write in the first person, you incorporate the narrator into the fabric of the story. In effect, the author becomes a character. Dostoevsky often does it; he writes a novel from the viewpoint of some character in a small town who never takes any part in the action, but who is the local chronicler—and that permits him to have editorial asides.)

The other difference between Hugo and me concerns a certain kind of repetition, which goes beyond what is necessary to convey the confusion of a priest confessing a guilty love to a girl. Some things are said over and over, in ways which do not fully add to the preceding.

Hugo's style consists in projecting above all the *emotion* involved. As a Romanticist of the first order, he knows that one does not project emotions qua emotions; he knows that emotions come from one's premises and one's evaluations of concretes. But he is much less concerned than I am with the intellectual meaning of the emotions he projects, and with the intellectual method of projecting them.

Of the two styles, mine is more masculine, if by "masculine" we mean a tight economy of intellectual content. Even if I write about violent emotions, I weigh every word for its direct meaning, for its connotations, for what it adds to the sentence. Mine is a more controlled presentation; Hugo's is much freer.

The second of the two passages I quoted from *Atlas Shrugged* was written inspirationally. It was written as I advise: write as it comes to you, then edit. But when I edit, I consider every word: "Is this word extraneous or necessary? Why do I want to keep it?" That particular passage I went over ten times, and few changes were made. But I could write it that way only because my premises were set to this kind of purposefulness and economy of expression; as a result, my subconscious did not produce much that was extraneous.

On other passages, my subconscious did not function as well—and that meant ten rewrites. I do not even have a manuscript page copied until I have made so many corrections on it that I can no longer use that sheet of paper; I experiment on the same page with ten different ways of wording a sentence. The reason is that I cannot compose a sentence word for word. I can only write it, then weigh it: "Sounds right. Why is it right?" If I can give the answer, it stays. If it is not quite right, why is it not? If I can grasp why, I rewrite it on the new premise. Sometimes I cannot grasp why, but the sentence simply does not sound right. Then I try writing it different ways, until I suddenly see: "Yes, this is what was missing."

Hugo would not work like this; as is obvious through all of his writing, he does not strive for such minute precision. It is as if his brushstrokes are wider and more "impressionistic" than mine, whereas while mine are wide, someone who approached them with a microscope would see that every strand was put there for a purpose.

Offhand, I will not say which method is better. It is a metaphysical issue. The fact that Hugo is consciously on the Christian-altruist code of values, and subconsciously not at all on it, is one reason why he would not look for extreme rational precision. That would not be part of his view of life, or, therefore, of his writing. Granting him his values and premises, his method is right for him.

In the above passages from *Atlas Shrugged* and *Notre-Dame de Paris*, the theme—the emotion of love—was conveyed by means of particulars chosen to represent the essence of that abstraction. This method is the essence of the Romantic approach to style.

The next passage, in contrast, is by Thomas Wolfe.

From *Of Time and the River* by Thomas Wolfe

Ah, strange and beautiful, the woman thought, how can I longer bear this joy intolerable, the music of this great song unpronounceable, the anguish of this glory unimaginable, which fills my life to bursting and which will not let me speak! . . . Oh magic moment that is so perfect, unknown, and inevitable, to stand here at this ship's great side, here at the huge last edge of evening and return, with this still wonder in my heart and knowing only that somehow we are fulfilled of you, oh time! . . . Ah secret and alone, she thought—how lean with hunger, and how fierce with pride, and how burning with impossible desire he bends there at the rail of night—and he is wild and young and foolish and forsaken, and his eyes are starved, his soul is parched with thirst, his heart is famished with a hunger that cannot be fed, and he leans there on the rail and dreams great dreams, and he is mad for love and is athirst for glory, and he is so cruelly mistaken—and so right! . . . Oh passionate and proud!—how like the wild, lost soul of youth you are, how like my wild lost father who will not return!

He turned, and saw her then, and so finding her, was lost, and so losing self, was found, and so seeing her, saw for a fading moment only the pleasant image of the woman that perhaps she was, and that life saw. He never knew: he only knew that from that moment his spirit was impaled upon the knife of love. From that moment on he never was again to lose her utterly, never to wholly re-possess unto himself the lonely, wild integrity of youth which had been his. At that instant of their meeting, that proud inviolability of youth was broken, not to be restored. At that moment of their meeting she got into his life by some dark magic, and before he knew it, he had her beating in the pulses of his blood—somehow thereafter—how he never knew—to steal into the conduits of his heart, and to inhabit the lone, inviolable tenement of his one life; so, like love's great thief, to steal through all

> the adyts of his soul, and to become a part of all he did and said and was—through this invasion so to touch all loveliness that he might touch, through this strange and subtle stealth of love henceforth to share all that he might feel or make or dream, until there was for him no beauty that she did not share, no music that did not have her being in it, no horror, madness, hatred, sickness of the soul, or grief unutterable, that was not somehow consonant to her single image and her million forms—and no final freedom and release, bought through the incalculable expenditure of blood and anguish and despair, that would not bear upon its brow forever the deep scar, upon its sinews the old mangling chains, of love.

One can gather that, on seeing each other for the first time, these two persons feel something violent for each other; at least the author's loud words convey that such was his *intention*. But he has not carried out his intention.

The reason is: floating abstractions. Take the first sentence. "*Ah, strange and beautiful, the woman thought.*" *What* is strange and beautiful? Is it life, or love, or the man she sees? "*How can I longer bear this joy intolerable, the music of this great song unpronounceable, the anguish of this glory unimaginable, which fills my life to bursting and which will not let me speak!*" One does not know the joy of *what*, the music of *what* song, *what* glory; one can only gather that the woman is feeling an emotion of some kind.

Wolfe is trying to convey an emotion directly, primarily by means of adjectives. You can observe here the unsatisfactory result of having adjectives without nouns and specific content—i.e., attributes without entities. One cannot convey the *quality* of something without conveying what that something *is*.

It is a bromide among editors that bad writing can be judged by the number of adjectives used. This is not an absolute standard, but it is true that beginners often use too many adjectives. Why? Because it is the easiest and laziest method of describing something. When Wolfe wrote "*joy intolerable*," "*song unpronounceable*," and "*glory unimaginable*," he evidently felt that if he put in *three* of these adjectives, they would somehow do something. Properly speaking, one would do—or ten, if each said something that contributed to the sentence.

Observe also the archaism of putting the adjective last: "*joy intolerable*," "*song unpronounceable*," "*glory unimaginable*." This is permissible when the content warrants it (there is nothing that one can *never* do in writing, unless it is irrational). But here the author attempts to substitute form for content: he attempts to convey the importance of the moment by substituting the *form* of an exalted feeling for the content which he has not conveyed.

In style, form follows function. If you convey the content of a strong emotion, you can use as loud a form as you wish because the content will support it. Similarly, if you wonder whether an adjective is superfluous, remember that you can do anything if your content permits it. But never substitute words for meaning.

Also, the easiest thing on earth is to call something "a song" or to speak about "the music" of something, "music" always connoting strong emotion. "Love is like music" or "architecture is music" or "poetry is music"—you have seen this ad nauseam. If warranted by the content, and if done in an original manner, it is permissible to compare something to music. But do not attempt to convey exaltation simply by saying "*the music of this great song*." What song?

Someone once told me that no writer should ever say "indescribable"—if it is not describable, then do not describe it. Here the author spends a whole sentence on "*song unpronounceable*," "*glory unimaginable*." When an author says, "This is unutterable," he is confessing inadequacy. It can have no other meaning; unutterable to whom? An author should not intrude his personal writing problems on the reader; the reader is following the events of the story, not the mechanics of the author's mind.

"*Oh magic moment that are so perfect, unknown, and inevitable*." Why is the moment "perfect," "unknown," and "inevitable"? There is no reason for these adjectives, except that they vaguely suggest something exalted or important. And what is meant by "*somehow we are fulfilled of you, oh time!*"? The author gives us the form of a sentence but no actual meaning; he is counting only on the *connotations* of the words. That is improper by the rules not only of literature, but of plain grammar.

Words are means of communication and must be used for their denotation. One of the beauties of a good literary style, as opposed to a dry synopsis, is that it combines clear denotation with the skillful use of connotation. But one can connote something only in relation to *something*. One cannot have connotations, which are relationships, without specifying any of the *entities* bearing these relationships.

"*Oh magic moment.*" It is permissible, and can be very effective, to use the word *oh* as an extreme expression of a particular emotion—when justified by the content. Observe that when Hugo used it—"*Oh, young girl, have pity on me!*"—there was a definite reason for the exclamation; the priest was appealing for pity. Here, by contrast, Wolfe uses the word *oh* merely to *describe* an emotion.

Also, never use the word *magic* in a positive sense. It is a lazy writer's word. To say that something is "magical" is too easy, just as mysticism is too easy a way out of philosophical problems. Mysticism is not at all easy psychologically, but it is, philosophically. Similarly, the word *magic* is not easy if you want to achieve a proper effect, but it is very easy literarily: if you do not know how to describe something, you say: "Oh, it's magical."

"*Ah secret and alone, she thought.*" The intention of this description is clear: the young man looks as if he has something secret about him. But to call him a "secret" man is an indefensible foreshortening. I do not mean that the author should have used an overprecise sentence like "The man looked as if he had a secret"; to be overprecise here would be out of the emotional key. And it *is* difficult to maintain clarity while conveying a strong emotional mood. But it is not proper to convey it by means of bad grammar. An old literary bromide says that when you write about boring people, you, the writer, do not have to be boring. The same applies here: you cannot convey an incoherent emotion by means of incoherent writing.

Incidentally, the one good line up to this point is in the preceding sentence: "*to stand here at this ship's great side, here at the huge last edge of evening and return.*" An evening and a return do not literally have an edge, but here one need not be grammatically pedantic. This whole passage is preceded by the description of a ship docking in the evening, and therefore the meaning of "*the huge last edge of evening and re-*

turn" is clear: the vastness of returning home in the evening. Here Wolfe does combine an emotion with a specific, physical description.

But then he repeats the same trick, very badly: "*he bends there at the rail of night.*" This is too foreshortened.

Next, the author states one idea three times by means of synonyms: "*his eyes are starved, his soul is parched with thirst, his heart is famished with a hunger that cannot be fed.*" This is an example of *not* writing by means of essences. If Wolfe wanted to convey the idea of spiritual hunger, and convey it *strongly*, his task was to find the strongest expression he could for such a hunger. His dilemma here was that none of these metaphors is strong enough by itself to convey what he wanted. But stating something three times does not make it stronger; it makes it three times weaker.

The last part of this sentence contains some specific meaning, and it is almost good: "*he is mad for love and is athirst for glory, and he is so cruelly mistaken—and so right!*" Here the author indicates what about the man impresses the woman. With direct simplicity, the sentence conveys her impression of him, her estimate of his future, and her philosophy (her view is that he is right to expect love and glory, but is destined for disappointment—which indicates a malevolent view of the universe on her part). The author says something specific, and he says it once. If, in the preceding, he had given some grounds for the woman's conclusion by describing the man's face or expression, this would have been a good sentence.

"*Oh passionate and proud!—how like the wild, lost soul of youth you are, how like my wild lost father who will not return!*" The reference to the woman's father spoils the emotional mood of the passage and destroys the preceding description of the young man, which emphasizes his youth, ambition, and future. A hymn to a woman's first meeting with her beloved cannot end on a *family recollection*. That is a real anticlimax.

Then the meeting is taken up from the standpoint of the young man. "*He turned, and saw her then, and so finding her, was lost, and so losing self, was found.*" Again, the author is playing for effect by means of words instead of content. It takes minutes to figure out what the sentence means: "Well, finding her, he was lost. How? Oh, by falling in love. Losing self, he was found. By whom?"

"He never knew: he only knew that from that moment his spirit was impaled upon the knife of love." This is an extremely ugly image: it connotes meat on a skewer or a soldier in a bad movie falling on a sword through his stomach. Admittedly, the metaphor is philosophical: the author regards love as a knife because it leads to disaster. But to make it so specific that one sees the man's spirit falling on that knife is inexcusably ugly.

"From that moment on he never was again to lose her utterly, never to wholly re-possess unto himself the lonely, wild integrity of youth which had been his." Observe the overuse of the word *wild*. It is bad to "ride" a word—to use it over and over, so that the reader becomes conscious of the repetition. In most books, editors have told me, the author rides some particular expression. Here, Wolfe does it within *one page*.

The above sentence does at least convey a specific thought: that this is the end of the man's youthful independence. But then the next sentence expresses exactly the same thought: "*At that instant of their meeting, that proud inviolability of youth was broken, not to be restored.*" Wolfe should have used one sentence or the other, but not both.

". . . henceforth to share all that he might feel or make or dream, until there was for him no beauty that she did not share, no music that did not have her being in it, no horror, madness, hatred, sickness of the soul, or grief unutterable, that was not somehow consonant to her single image and her million forms." The thought is good: the woman will hereafter be part of every important moment of the man's life. It is also good that Wolfe tries to specify the moments; here he is writing by means of essential details. But the terrible overwriting destroys the dignity of the thought: "*horror, madness, hatred, sickness of the soul, or grief unutterable.*" A writer has to know when to stop.

The best part of this sentence is: "*that was not somehow consonant to her single image and her million forms.*" Wolfe has communicated not only his meaning, but also its emotional quality. To have said "her personality and its different aspects" would have been a dry synopsis; "*her single image and her million forms*" is both specific and Romantic. But to reach the meaning of the emotion Wolfe is conveying, the reader has to break through some dreadful verbal weeds.

"—and no final freedom and release, bought through the incalculable expenditure of blood and anguish and despair, that would not bear upon its

brow forever the deep scar, upon its sinews the old mangling chains, of love." Wolfe is trying to suggest some great suffering, but it cannot be done by piling up synonyms. Never use words like *blood, anguish*, and *despair* together; one means essentially the same as the others. And if you mean despair, then *anguish* is too weak a word; if you mean blood, then both *anguish* and *despair* are anticlimaxes.

What kind of philosophy comes across in Wolfe's style? First, a malevolent view of the universe, which he reveals not merely in such particular statements as "*he is so cruelly mistaken*," but in the whole tone of "This is torture, but it's wonderful," "This is fate, and we're helpless." Inherent in his style is an implication of human helplessness in the face of emotion and destiny.

But the main philosophical implication of Wolfe's style is subjectivism. A man who approached reality objectively would not write this way; he would not, for instance, relate what the two persons saw in each other without giving any indication of the physical means by which they inferred it all. Wolfe, however, does not identify what causes his own emotions, and therefore has no idea how to communicate those emotions to others; all he knows is that certain semipoetic expressions appeal to him, and he tries to communicate emotions by means of these. They are not the proper means.

In this whole passage from Wolfe, there is a very meager selection of content and an enormous overweight of language. The content could be conveyed in two sentences; the rest is extra words. This is not to say that a first meeting between lovers must be described in two sentences. No, you can write four pages on it—if you have something to say.

Thomas Wolfe's style is the archetype of what I call, borrowing from modern sculpture, the "mobile" style: it is so vague that anyone can interpret it as anything he wishes. This is why his appeal is usually to people under twenty. Wolfe presents an empty mold to be filled by any reader, the general intention being aspiration, undefined idealism, the desire to escape from the commonplace and to find "something better in Life"—none of it given any content. A young reader recognizes the intention and supplies his own concretes—if he does not hold the writer responsible for conveying his own meaning, but is willing to take him merely as a springboard.

I cannot do that. I do not collaborate with what I read in any such manner.

From *Arrowsmith* by Sinclair Lewis

Sound of mating birds, sound of spring blossoms dropping in the tranquil air, the bark of sleepy dogs at midnight; who is to set them down and make them anything but hackneyed? And as natural, as conventional, as youthfully gauche, as eternally beautiful and authentic as those ancient sounds was the talk of Martin and Leora in that passionate half-hour when each found in the other a part of his own self, always vaguely missed, discovered now with astonished joy. They rattled like hero and heroine of a sticky tale, like sweat-shop operatives, like bouncing rustics, like prince and princess. Their words were silly and inconsequential, heard one by one, yet taken together they were as wise and important as the tides or the sounding wind.

The purpose of this passage, which follows the first meeting of Martin and Leora, is to present the essence of their romance.

"*Sound of mating birds, sound of spring blossoms dropping in the tranquil air, the bark of sleepy dogs at midnight; who is to set them down and make them anything but hackneyed?*" Here the author openly confesses incompetence, saying in effect: "I have only the hackneyed to say about this, but that's in the nature of things. Nobody could do otherwise." Not all Naturalists reveal their writing problems by telling the reader about them (which is improper from any literary standpoint); nevertheless, it is the Naturalist premise that makes Lewis do it. On the Naturalist premise, a writer describes "things as they are," not things as they ought to be. The method of selection is not a value judgment, but a statistical one. Consequently, when Lewis wants to present a setting or connotation proper to love, he will think only of the hackneyed—which is the statistically average.

"*And as natural, as conventional, as youthfully gauche, as eternally beautiful and authentic as those ancient sounds was the talk of Martin and Leora.*" Here Lewis confesses the Naturalist premise: "This is hackneyed, but it is natural and authentic." Natural and authentic to whom? As a Naturalist, he does not ask this question. He describes love from the statistical viewpoint.

His fidelity to what he thinks is reality—meaning: the statistical and the average—is also obvious when he says "*youthfully gauche*." The majority of young lovers may be youthfully gauche, but that is not a law of human nature. I submit that any outstanding young people are *more* romantic and dramatically outspoken than they become later on. Yet the kind of young man or girl who will say, "Oh, gee, darling, you know, I'm kind of smitten," *that* is Lewis's (and Hollywood's) idea of young love.

Calling this "*eternally beautiful*" is again a confession of the statistical standard. "This is what most lovers act like; and, of course, love is beautiful; therefore, this is its beautiful form." The Naturalist does not project the values which *ought* to be, and so he presents love not in its highest form, but strictly in its statistical form.

The last part of this sentence is good in that it says something specific (and true) about the nature of love: "*each found in the other a part of his own self, always vaguely missed, discovered now with astonished joy*." This is specific—and general. It pertains to the essence of love more than do "*mating birds*" and "*spring blossoms*."

The next sentence is the writing of a repressor. "*They rattled like hero and heroine of a sticky tale, like sweat-shop operatives, like bouncing rustics, like prince and princess*." Lewis wants to convey that love is important and that a romance is happening between Martin and Leora, but at the same time he is apologizing to any cynical "realist" who is not in sympathy with romantic feeling. He in effect says: "Romantic scenes might be accused by the sophisticated of being sticky. All right, I'll admit it, I'll smile at it myself—so don't take it too seriously. But still I consider love important." To make the scene more "true to life," he then selects the lowest possible forms of couples: "*sweat-shop operatives*" and "*bouncing rustics*." He in effect acknowledges: "By the statistical standard, there are more sweat-shop operatives and bouncing rustics than princes and princesses, so I'll include them. I am paying my dues to reality. But still Martin and Leora *were* like a prince and princess, or at least that is how they felt."

The last sentence is again the confession of a writer's impotence: "*Their words were silly and inconsequential, heard one by one, yet taken together they were as wise and important as the tides or the sounding wind.*" Lovers usually have a kidding romantic code which might be silly objectively, but which has meaning to the two persons subjectively. This phenomenon is one of the hardest things for any writer to communicate on paper, so Lewis solves the problem by saying *descriptively*: "Yes, the individual words are probably silly, but the sum is important because it expresses intimacy and love." This is inexcusable literarily. A writer who wants to be true to reality should undertake here to convey the romantic code of lovers. It would be difficult, but it can be done.

Observe that the two Romantics I have presented, and the in-between case of Thomas Wolfe, all made a big to-do (to put it in Sinclair Lewis's style) about the issue of love; they focused on it in detail. By contrast, Lewis spends pages describing Martin's school and Leora's hospital [he is a medical student and she a nurse]; then, when the Naturalist comes to that which makes life important—their first romance—he gives it a short, semisatirical paragraph. This is not an accident. Not all Naturalists are as inhibited as Lewis, who has a quality here of the repressed Romantic, but the essence of their method is always the same.

From *Star Money* by Kathleen Winsor

They went into his room and took off their clothes, smiling at each other and without self-consciousness. Johnny was undressed first and he lay down on the bed, his hands behind his head, watching her. Shireen turned, stepped out of her petticoat and faced him. Her eyes had turned dark and her face lapsed into sudden serious intensity, as if she wondered how he would find her; but also as if she had lost Shireen Delaney and came toward him only as a woman, a part of time and every woman who ever lived. She sat beside him on the bed, leaning forward, one hand lifting and moving to touch his hair. He reached out and took hold of her and all at once he grinned.

"Chocolate cake with peppermint frosting—that's you." His hands touched her breasts lightly. "You're all the favors wrapped up in one package."

Shireen gave a sudden triumphant ringing laugh and he pulled her down against him.

This passage is typical of what is known as "magazine writing." The words are completely inconsequential; the style, lacking any emotional or intellectual significance, is merely one step above a plain synopsis. The particular quality of magazine writing is that almost anything can be said or can happen.

The author does show—I assume, unintentionally—what love means to the woman in the scene. In a moment of passion, all she is thinking about is how the man will find her when she takes off her clothes; and when he finds her to be a chocolate cake, she gives a triumphant ringing laugh. She passed the test. All that love means to this woman is reassurance to her ego—a self-esteem derived from somebody else's appreciation.

The description here is totally meaningless and unemotional—but then the author apparently remembers that she is writing a love scene and that something important has to be said. So she slings some tired, superficial generalities: "*as if she had lost Shireen Delaney and came toward him only as a woman, a part of time and every woman who ever lived.*" I think she was trying to say something like "This is love, which would have the same meaning for every woman in every time." Then, having done her duty by love's significance, she goes back to the magazine style: "*She sat beside him on the bed, leaning forward, one hand lifting and moving to touch his hair.*"

The dialogue is Naturalism (if one can call it anything at all) in that the author is using what she considers realistic slang. She probably thought: "This is how a real he-man talks." Of course, nobody talks like that, not even in a bad Hollywood movie. (Even magazine fiction is not *that* ridiculous.)

If you ever attempt to write without full awareness of what you are saying, why you are saying it, and what you are writing about, this will be the result. This is somebody who is writing in a half-dazed state, not projecting the reality or the emotional or intellectual meaning of her subject matter, but merely slinging words together while drawing on the subconscious residue of her impressions of similar scenes from other stories.

From *By Love Possessed* by James Gould Cozzens

In recollection's light, first to be noted was the plain fact that, by standards of what was later learned, the feelings affording a young man his state of love, of being in love, were largely factitious. This was not by any means to say that they were false or pretended; but, still, they had not, as the young man himself was likely to imagine, arisen spontaneously. In theory, the feelings resulted when love magically and mysteriously seized on him; in theory, that was what love did. In practice, love did nothing of the kind. He, the truth usually was, seized on love. A young man heard and read of a thing called love. Love was praised everywhere as pure, noble, and beautiful. Love *did* have to do with the commerce between the sexes; but love as described clearly could not have to do with sex—the physical urges of nature that he knew about. Those had been denounced to him as evil and impure, the associates of what he joined in calling (even if he fairly frequently indulged in them) dirty jokes, dirty thoughts, dirty practices. What those were, must be everything true love wasn't. Love knew them not. Love, manifestly, was out of this world. Love's high feelings, at once so exciting and so presentable, could, moreover, be had, apparently, by anyone. A young man would not be long in resolving to have some. . . .

. . . To the rules of high-mindedness, the flesh is imperfectly amenable. Kisses however chaste, caresses however decent, if the exchange of them is kept up, must have the flesh soon shaping to its natural end, projecting its actual objective. A discipline of mind was required. The witching hour was to be saved intact by a division of consciousness; one part excluding rigidly all that engaged the other part. Held separate, thoughts on the plane of moonlight and roses could proceed regardless of the lower animal. Or, at least, they could so proceed to a point. Due to that blameless neglect of Hope's to call the halt she (the fair, the chaste, the inexpressive she!) had no need to call; and to her partner in petting's reluctance to leave, since he was free to remain, there had been awkward occasions when the animal (disregarded by the hour and teased too far) reacted of a sudden, put to the shilly-shally so long imposed its own unpreventable end. Arthur Winner Junior—confusion in the moonlight; dismay among the roses!—was obliged to conceal as well as he could a crisis about which his single shamed consolation was that Hope, anything but knowing, would never know what had happened.

This is not an unselective, unvaluing recording. The author's value judgments are obvious. Yet it is intended as a Naturalistic recording of "things as they are."

Observe all the slanted writing. For instance, the author describes *as a fact of nature* the hero's attitude toward love. He does not say that this was the attitude of a particular young man—he describes it in generalized terms, as if all young men fall in love only because they have heard about it. "*A young man heard and read of a thing called love. Love was praised everywhere as pure, noble, and beautiful.*" Since love is praised, according to the author, a young man will be motivated by such praise.

All young men *in fact* feel nothing, Cozzens implies; they merely tell themselves they feel something because they hear that other people feel it. This amounts to saying that the psychology of all young men is ten times worse than what I presented, in *The Fountainhead*, in the character of Peter Keating.

"*Love as described clearly could not have to do with sex—the physical urges of nature that he knew about. Those had been denounced to him as evil and impure.*" This is a false and awful view of sex—the Christian-mystical view. Cozzens presents the most vicious code of values—man is helpless, sex is a stupid physical urge belonging to his lower animal nature, his "high" feelings are merely a silly romantic illusion—yet he does not state that this is the view of his hero or of the hero's social group. These value judgments are the ones conventionally held by most people, Cozzens believes, and so he does not consider them estimates. He considers them facts of human nature.

The two elements which constitute style are content (what an author chooses to say) and use of words (the way he says it). Not only is what Cozzens says about man and love horrible; there is something extremely repulsive about the manner in which he says it. If one were to identify the essence of his style in one word, that word would be *sneer*. Cozzens is sneering—at love, and at man as such.

Observe his repetitions, which are not accidental (nor are they as innocent as those of Thomas Wolfe, who repeated things for poetic or rhythmical purposes). At the beginning, he says: "*the feelings affording a young man his state of love, of being in love, were largely factitious.*" He uses the phrase "*state of love,*" which is a formal statement of his subject, then adds the colloquial "*being in love.*" Why? In order to sneer at the reader on the side: "If you're so stupid that you don't know what the 'state of love' is, I am making fun of that state which you will recognize better as 'being in love.' " (The repetition also adds another element: awkwardness; deliberately planned awkwardness.)

"*In theory, the feelings resulted when love magically and mysteriously seized on him; in theory, that was what love did.*" The purpose of this repetition is again to imply the stupidity of the reader. Cozzens is saying: "In theory, love does such and such. In theory, that's what love does. You can't get a thought the first time, so I'll tell it to you with a patronizing sneer a second time."

Cozzens claims that love, in theory, comes magically out of nowhere, and then he says: "*In practice, love did nothing of the kind.*" Since "theory" here means reason or thought, the implied conclusion is that man is unable to think.

This is a good example of how the alleged opposition between theory and practice is always presented. A foolish and illogical theory is first set up, and then the author triumphantly shows that it does not work in practice. In this passage, Cozzens takes the tritest, most superficial of theories—that love is blind—and proceeds to say that it is not so. His purpose—and the purpose of the whole theory-practice opposition—is to show that man's mind is impotent to deal with reality or with his own emotions. A man believed one thing about love and, in reality, found something else. The question to ask is: If he believed the kind of nonsense which Cozzens presents, is the fault in man's mind or in this particular man's foolishness? But Cozzens does not ask that question. His intention is the undercutting of the mind and the degradation of man.

The next stylistic trait to observe is Cozzens's stodgy writing style—a satire on the long, involved, awkward sentences of mid-Victorian novels—which he intersperses with deliberately vulgar bromides like "*moonlight and roses,*" "*the lower animal,*" and "*out of this world.*" They are included to remind the reader that "I, the author, am now condescending to speak your language, which would be 'moonlight and roses' and 'out of this world.' " The implication is that the reader will not understand such ponderous talk as "*manifestly*" or "*state of love*" or "*commerce between the sexes*," so the author will let his hair down once in a while with vulgarities which the reader *will* understand. This deliberate use of ugly, inexpressive bromides in the middle of the awkward archaic style is one reason why the writing is so unattractive. And it is another means for Cozzens to convey his metaphysical sneer.

The style of this quotation will make any sensitive reader uncomfortable. The insult to his intelligence is built into the sentences; it is there in the choice both of what the author says and of the way he says it.

One cannot grasp the author's meaning at the first reading, not because his style is so subtle and profound, but because it is so involved grammatically. For instance: "*Due to that blameless neglect of Hope's to call the halt she (the fair, the chaste, the inexpressive she!) had no need to call; and to her partner in petting's reluctance to leave, since he was free to remain, there had been awkward occasions when the animal (disregarded by the hour and teased too far) reacted of a sudden, put to the shilly-shally so long imposed its own unpreventable end.*" This is not bad writing in the sense that Cozzens could not do any better; it is good writing by his standard, i.e., it is what he intended, and it probably took hard work, because no one writes like this naturally. If by "art" we mean an intention purposefully carried out, this is high art. What one can quarrel with is the intention.

The intention is the deliberate destruction of the reader's mental efficacy. The grammatical structures make it impossible for the reader to follow a thought. "*Due to that blameless neglect of Hope's to call the halt she (the fair, the chaste, the inexpressive she!) had no need to call.*" By phrasing the sentence differently, the author could have left the reader grammatical time to remember the character of Hope, then said what Hope failed to do—which would have been the logical order. Instead, he interrupts the thought at the most awkward point, between the subject and the verb, *she* and *had*. Why? Precisely to throw the reader off for a moment; i.e., not to allow his mind to proceed to a complete thought.

He does the same in the second half of the sentence: "*there had been awkward occasions when the animal (disregarded by the hour and teased too far) reacted of a sudden.*" For the reader to grasp it, a thought has to progress in a certain time sequence; but here the author again interrupts in the middle of the thought, throwing the reader into an aside and making him scramble mentally to catch the original intention. Cozzens deliberately puts the reader's mind into an unfocused, nonrational state of wandering all over the map.

One has to watch carefully the between-the-lines implications to know what Cozzens is actually talking about in this sentence. In this respect, he is imitating the special kind of mid-Victorian prissiness which consists of being very bashfully indirect in talking about sex—and the more indirect, the dirtier the implications of what one dares not say openly.

What he is doing is illustrating the theory of love expressed in the first part of the quotation. That is, even though the young man had decided that love has nothing to do with sex, and even though the young couple tried to keep their relationship chaste, things would happen against the young man's will; and Cozzens does not mean normal intercourse. The style of this—the mere fact that he is not talking about an actual affair, but about something totally unnecessary to mention—makes this passage typical of Cozzens. Writing in the spiritual style of four-letter words, he goes out of his way to make something ugly which is not necessarily ugly at all.

The best-drawn character in anyone's writing is the author himself. None of the above passages deals with philosophy directly, yet the author's philosophy is present—in what he chooses to say and in how he says it. In this sense, a fiction writer cannot hide himself. He stands naked spiritually.

You cannot create a style artificially, composing each sentence word by word and then weighing each word: "How does this fit with my official dogma?" A writer's style comes from his *accepted* philosophy—accepted in his subconscious.

Just as, in your general behavior as a human being, your premises "will out"—they will come out in many subtle ways, and any conflict you might have will show, particularly in emergencies—so in your writing your premises will out. If your conscious philosophy has sunk into your subconscious and become automatic, that will show in your style. If your conscious philosophy is not fully assimilated—if you have premises contradictory to it in your subconscious—that will show. If you have good premises, that will show. If you have god-awful premises, then, in the passage from Cozzens, you have just seen an example of the result.

If you are not satisfied with what comes out of your subconscious, you can correct it by conscious thinking. But do not censor yourself in the process of writing. That cannot be done successfully. To be the kind of writer you want to be, you must first be the kind of thinker you want to be.

Just as man is a being of self-made soul, so a writer is a being of self-made style. Both are made by the same process—by a man's being fully convinced of certain premises to the point where they become subconscious and automatic.

9

Style II: Descriptions of Nature and of New York

From *Atlas Shrugged* by Ayn Rand

She sat at the window of the train, her head thrown back, not moving, wishing she would never have to move again.

The telegraph poles went racing past the window, but the train seemed lost in a void, between a brown stretch of prairie and a solid spread of rusty, graying clouds. The twilight was draining the sky without the wound of a sunset; it looked more like the fading of an anemic body in the process of exhausting its last drops of blood and light. The train was going west, as if it, too, were pulled to follow the sinking rays and quietly to vanish from the earth. She sat still, feeling no desire to resist it.

This description illustrates the art of combining denotation and connotation.

My assignment was to describe a sunset seen from the window of a train—a dismal sunset that would match Dagny's mood in this scene. I give the reader precise information about the sight by means of those details which convey its essence; and I convey the *mood* by the kind of words and metaphor I select. Unlike Thomas Wolfe, I do not try to convey the mood apart from that which creates the mood. Instead, I carefully select words that both convey the exact physical details *and* have specific connotations.

For instance, in the phrase "*a solid spread of rusty, graying clouds*," the word *rusty* conveys not only the color, but also something dismal. In the next sentence, the word *twilight* has connotations of sadness. And the best part of this description is: "*The twilight was draining the sky without the wound of a sunset.*" Since a sunset *would* look like a wound across the sky, the metaphor is visually appropriate and helps the reader visualize a sunset; and by saying that the sky was being drained *without* the wound of a sunset, I convey, by means of a negative, both the exact description and the mood. Then I continue the metaphor in the same style: "*it looked more like the fading of an anemic body in the process of exhausting its last drops of blood and light.*" When I say "*and light*," I bring the metaphor back to the concrete reality of the sunset and the evening.

Suppose I had started by saying: "It was evening and she sat at the window of a train. The twilight was draining the sky without the wound of a sunset." That would have been a floating abstraction. I first have to give specific details: there is a brown stretch of prairie, the sky is covered with clouds, they are of a rusty shade so that one would not see the sun setting. Then the metaphor "*without the wound of a sunset*" becomes convincing. To start with such a metaphor would be vague and unclear, because the question would be: Where did the sunset go?

In the next sentence, the words all have a downbeat, twilight feeling. "*The train was going west*"—this connotes the sunset and evening—"*as if it, too, were pulled*"—it is not even going of its own power—"*to follow the sinking rays and quietly to vanish from the earth.*" This is a literal description, since the train *is* going west, but by saying "*quietly to vanish from the earth*," I imply more than merely vanishing into the sunset. I imply destruction and hopelessness, and the feeling of "your days are numbered," which is the emotional key of this chapter.

According to my metaphysical view, nature is of interest to a human being only as his material or setting. I therefore always describe nature as a background for man, never as an end in itself considered separately from the characters or the scene taking place. (This is a point open to debate. If a writer attaches some special value to the description of nature, I would say that he has a wrong premise; but one could not say that, in carrying out his premise, he is guilty of overwriting.)

The above description is written from Dagny's viewpoint; she is sitting at the window of a train, and this is what she sees. However, observe that I could have written the same description without referring to anyone sitting at a window, since I describe what the place and the sunset actually *look* like. I do not project Dagny's emotions into the description.

When we come to the last quotation, from Thomas Wolfe, you will see a different approach. In his description of New York, he does not differentiate between what is being seen and what the character feels.

From *Seven Gothic Tales* by Isak Dinesen

The road from Closter Seven to Hopballehus rises more than five hundred feet and winds through tall pine forest. From time to time this opens and affords a magnificent view over large stretches of land below. Now in the afternoon sun the trunks of the fir trees were burning red, and the landscape far away seemed cool, all blue and pale gold. Boris was able now to believe what the old gardener at the convent had told him when he was a child: that he had once seen, about this time of the year and the day, a herd of unicorns come out of the woods to graze upon the sunny slopes, the white and dappled mares, rosy in the sun, treading daintily and looking around for their young, the old stallion, darker roan, sniffing and pawing the ground. The air here smelled of fir leaves and toadstools, and was so fresh that it made him yawn. And yet, he thought, it was different from the freshness of spring; the courage and gaiety of it were tinged with despair. It was the finale of the symphony.

This is one of the most beautiful descriptions I have read in the Romantic style. (Primarily a writer of fantastic stories, Isak Dinesen is hard to classify; but she is certainly nearer to being a Romanticist than a Naturalist.)

First the author gives a general idea of the setting: it is a winding road rising through pine forest. Then she begins to give particulars: "*Now in the afternoon sun the trunks of the fir trees were burning red, and the landscape far away seemed cool, all blue and pale gold.*" By means of a few essentials, the reader gets an attractive generalized picture.

The author then does something unusual and difficult. To convey the mood of the landscape and to give the reader a wider, more essential impression of it than she could have done by describing more leaves or branches or grass, she introduces this peculiar device: "*Boris was able now to believe what the old gardener at the convent had told him when he was a child: that he had once seen, about this time of the year and the day, a herd of unicorns come out of the woods to graze upon the sunny slopes.*" Observe the connotations. That an old gardener at a convent tells something to a child has in itself a fantastic quality; and when he tells him that he has seen unicorns, this impossible fantasy projects the exact eerie quality of the afternoon. "A herd of horses" would not have produced the same effect, because the purpose is to suggest something supernatural, odd, almost decadently frightening, but very attractive. The words "*about this time of the year and the day*" skillfully show the author's intention: it is not to indulge in a fantasy for its own sake, but to convey that at this time of year and day, the sunlight on these trees and this slope has the eerie, fantastic quality that could make one expect the supernatural.

As the author goes on to describe the unicorns, they are made specific in an unusually artistic way. The description is almost overdetailed, but by essentials: "*the white and dappled mares, rosy in the sun, treading daintily and looking around for their young, the old stallion, darker roan, sniffing and pawing the ground.*" Observe how carefully the color scheme is projected: that the mares are "*white and dappled*" but "*rosy in the sun*" is another reminder of the late afternoon sunlight. That they are "*treading daintily*" connotes the steps of elegant racehorses; yet the mares are unicorns, which makes them even more dainty. This amount of detail gives reality to the fantastic; and by so doing, the author conveys the mood of the afternoon.

The next sentence is completely realistic: "*The air here smelled of fir leaves and toadstools, and was so fresh that it made him yawn.*" It is a brilliant sentence: with great economy of words, the very essentials are selected so that one can almost *smell* the forest.

"*And yet, he thought, it was different from the freshness of spring; the courage and gaiety of it were tinged with despair.*" Since the freshness is different from that of spring, one can infer that it is fall. But what would imply, without the author saying it, that this is fall, is all the eerie fantasy that has gone before: the air of something supernatural, in gold, pink, red shades—the air of something decadent. The last sentence sums up the whole effect: "*It was the finale of the symphony.*"

The author has given a specific description of this hillside and no other—at this time of year and day. To convey the mood, she gives specific images, such as the fir trees, the unicorns, their colors and gestures, and even the perspective, and the smell of the forest. These are concretes, as distinguished from: "It was an eerie, fantastic landscape; beautiful but tragic; lovely but heartbreaking." Those would be floating abstractions.

From *The Fountainhead* by Ayn Rand

> From the train, he looked back once at the skyline of the city as it flashed into sight and was held for some moments beyond the windows. The twilight had washed off the details of the buildings. They rose in thin shafts of a soft, porcelain blue, a color not of real things, but of evening and distance. They rose in bare outlines, like empty molds waiting to be filled. The distance had flattened the city. The single shafts stood immeasurably tall, out of scale to the rest of the earth. They were of their own world, and they held up to the sky the statement of what man had conceived and made possible. They were empty molds. But man had come so far; he could go farther. The city on the edge of the sky held a question—and a promise.

Here I present first a visual description by means of essentials and then the symbolic or philosophical meaning of that description.

The first part of this passage describes the city, the second part conveys the meaning. The two are tied together by the concept of "*empty molds,*" which is legitimate in both contexts. "*They rose in bare outlines, like empty molds waiting to be filled.*" This is what buildings do look like at a distance, when the details are not seen. The transition to the philosophical meaning is done in this sentence: "*The single shafts stood immeasurably tall, out of scale to the rest of the earth. They were of their own world*"—this could apply both to their size and their meaning—"*and they held up to the sky the statement of what man had conceived and made possible. They were empty molds. But man had come so far; he could go farther.*" Here, "*empty molds*" is used strictly in the symbolic sense, to represent a promise.

This passage comes at the end of Part I of *The Fountainhead*, when Roark has to leave the city to work in the granite quarry. The meaning of the passage is therefore clear: "*The city on the edge of the sky held a question—and a promise.*" A *question* since Roark, given his position, cannot be sure of what the future holds; a *promise* since man (meaning Roark) "*could go farther.*"

What I am conveying here is the inspirational quality of the sight of the city—inspirational to Roark in the particular context of the novel; and inspirational in a wider sense, since I stress that the city is a symbol of human achievement.

This passage illustrates the method by which you can integrate, yet keep separately clear, a physical description and its philosophical meaning. Observe that the meaning is legitimately derived from the description. After describing tall buildings that rise above and out of scale to the rest of the earth, the conclusion that they represent the shape of human achievement is logically justified. (Again, keep this in mind when we come to the last quotation, from Thomas Wolfe, which follows a different method.)

From *Atlas Shrugged* by Ayn Rand

[The following analysis of a paragraph from *Atlas Shrugged*, originally given in connection with this course, was later written out by Ayn Rand herself. It is reprinted here as written (except for minor changes in punctuation).]

Clouds had wrapped the sky and had descended as fog to wrap the streets below, as if the sky were engulfing the city. She could see the whole of Manhattan Island, a long, triangular shape cutting into an invisible ocean. It looked like the prow of a sinking ship; a few tall buildings still rose above it, like funnels, but the rest was disappearing under gray-blue coils, going down slowly into vapor and space. This was how they had gone—she thought—Atlantis, the city that sank into the ocean, and all the other kingdoms that vanished, leaving the same legend in all the languages of men, and the same longing.

This description had four purposes: (1) to give an image of the view from Dagny's window, namely, an image of what New York looks like on a foggy evening; (2) to suggest the meaning of the events which have been taking place, namely, the city as a symbol of greatness doomed to destruction; (3) to connect New York with the legend of Atlantis; (4) to convey Dagny's mood. So the description had to be written on four levels: literal, connotative, symbolic, emotional.

The opening sentence of the description sets the key for all four levels: "*Clouds had wrapped the sky and had descended as fog to wrap the streets below, as if the sky were engulfing the city.*" On the literal level, the sentence is exact: it describes a foggy evening. But had I said something like "There were clouds in the sky, and the streets were full of fog," the sentence would have achieved nothing more. By casting the sentence into an active form, by wording it as if the clouds were pursuing some goal, I achieve the following: (1) on the literal level, a more graphic image of the view, because the sentence suggests the motion, the progressive thickening of the fog; (2) on the connotative level, it suggests the conflict of two adversaries and the grandeur of the conflict, since the adversaries are *sky* and *city*, and it suggests that the city is doomed, since it is being engulfed; (3) on the symbolic level, the word *engulfing* strikes the keynote for the tie to Atlantis, suggesting the act of sinking and, by connotation, blending the motion of the fog with the motion of waves; (4) on the emotional level, the use of so quiet a verb as *to wrap* in the context of an ominous, *engulfing* conflict establishes a mood of quiet, desolate hopelessness.

"*She could see the whole of* Manhattan Island, *a long, triangular shape cutting into an invisible ocean.*" This sentence is a literal, realistic description—but by the words "*cutting into an invisible ocean,*" I prepare the way for the comparison in the next sentence, I mention the word *ocean* as another link to Atlantis, and the fact that it is an *invisible* ocean does two things: conveys the density of the actual fog and suggests the symbolic, legendary meaning.

"*It looked like the prow of a sinking ship; a few tall buildings still rose above it, like funnels, but the rest was disappearing under gray-blue coils, going down slowly into vapor and space.*" Here I allow my purpose to come out into the open, but since it is prepared for, it reads like a legitimate, unforced description of a view. Yet it accomplishes the following: (1) on the literal level, a good description of the view of New York, since it is specific enough to be sensuously real; (2) on the connotative level, "*a few tall buildings still rose above it*" suggests the heroic, the few lone fighters holding out against that to which all the lesser elements have succumbed; (3) on the symbolic level, the tie between a "*sinking*" ship and a sinking city is obvious; "*disappearing under gray-blue coils*" applies equally to coils of fog or to the waves of an ocean; "*going down slowly into vapor and space*" is my integration of all four levels, slanted just enough to make the reader notice it: the word *vapor* still ties the sentence to the literal description of the fog, but the thought of "going down slowly into space" cannot actually apply to the view nor to a sinking ship, it applies to the destruction of New York and to Atlantis, that is, to the vanishing of greatness, of the ideal; (4) the emotional mood is obvious.

"*This was how they had gone—she thought—Atlantis, the city that sank into the ocean, and all the other kingdoms that vanished, leaving the same legend in all the languages of men, and the same longing.*" This is the conclusion of the description, the "cashing-in" sentence; it is not brought in arbitrarily, but sums up the meaning of the elements which the reader has been given in the preceding three sentences, to form, in effect, the following impression in the reader's mind: "Yes, I see why she would feel that way."

The above are merely the main considerations that went into the writing of this paragraph. There were many, many other considerations directing the choice and placement of every single word; it would take pages to list them all.

As an example, let us take the last sentence and try to rewrite it.

Suppose I changed it to: "This is how Atlantis had gone, she thought." This would have been jarring and artificial, since it would have picked up Dagny's thoughts too conveniently and directly on the subject of *Atlantis*, in the form of a full, pat sentence. The words with which I actually begin the sentence, "*This was how they had gone—she thought,*" serve as a bridge from the description of the view to introspection, to Dagny's thoughts—and suggest that the thought of Atlantis came to her suddenly, involuntarily, by emotional association rather than by conscious deliberation.

Suppose I reduced that sentence to a mere mention of Atlantis and of nothing else. This would have left the real meaning of the whole paragraph to implication—a vague, optional implication which the reader would not necessarily notice. By saying "*and all the other kingdoms that vanished,*" I made my main purpose explicitly clear: that the paragraph refers to that lost ideal which mankind had always been pursuing, struggling for, seeking and never finding.

Suppose I had ended the sentence on "*leaving the same legend in all the languages of men.*" This would have made it merely a thought of an historical nature, with no emotional meaning for Dagny and no indication of the emotional cause that brought this particular thought to her mind. The interpretation of her emotional reaction would then have been left at the mercy of any particular reader's subjective inclinations: it could have been sadness, fear, anger, hopelessness, or nothing in particular. By adding the words "*and the same longing,*" I indicated her specific mood and the essence of her emotional reaction to her present situation in the world: a desperate longing for an ideal that has become unattainable.

Suppose I rewrote the end of the sentence in a different order, thus: "and all the other kingdoms that vanished, leaving the same legend and the same longing in all the languages of men." This would have placed the emphasis on the universality of the quest for the ideal, on the fact that it is shared by all mankind. But what I wanted to emphasize was the quest for the ideal, not its universality; therefore, the words "*and the same longing*" had to be featured, had to come last, almost as a painfully reluctant confession and a climax.

No, I do not expect the reader of that paragraph to grasp consciously all the specific considerations listed above. I expect him to get a general impression, an emotional sum—the particular sum I intended. A reader has to be concerned only with the end result; unless he chooses to analyze it, he does not have to know by what means that result was achieved—but it is *my* job to know.

No, I did not calculate all this by a conscious process of thought while writing that paragraph. I will not attempt here to explain the whole psychological complexity of the process of writing; I will merely indicate its essence: it consists of giving one's subconscious the right orders in advance, or of setting the right premises. One must hold all the basic elements of the book's theme, plot, and main characters so firmly in one's mind that they become automatic and almost "instinctual." Then, as one approaches the actual writing of any given scene or paragraph, one has a sense or "feel" of what it has to be by the logic of the context—and one's subconscious makes the right selections to express it. Later, one checks and improves the result by means of conscious editing.

From *One Lonely Night* by Mickey Spillane

Nobody ever walked across the bridge, not on a night like this. The rain was misty enough to be almost fog-like, a cold gray curtain that separated me from the pale ovals of white that were faces locked behind the steamed-up windows of the cars that hissed by. Even the brilliance that was Manhattan by night was reduced to a few sleepy, yellow lights off in the distance.

Some place over there I had left my car and started walking, burying my head in the collar of my raincoat, with the night pulled in around me like a blanket. I walked and I smoked and I flipped the spent butts ahead of me and watched them arch to the pavement and fizzle out with one last wink. If there was life behind the windows of the buildings on either side of me, I didn't notice it. The street was mine, all mine. They gave it to me gladly and wondered why I wanted it so nice and all alone.

This is Romantic writing: the author selects the essentials (and does so very well).

For instance, when a man is walking alone in the rain, there are a great many sights around him: wet pavements, streetlights, tin cans, garbage pails. But what is most typical of the setting the author wants to establish? The faces in the cars—"*the pale ovals of white that were faces locked behind the steamed-up windows of the cars that hissed by.*" Where a lesser writer would have said merely "the faces," Spillane describes the way they would actually be seen; it is exactly what those faces would look like under the circumstances: "*pale ovals of white.*" The words "*locked behind the steamed-up windows*" are very artistic: that would be one's impression of faces going by in small compartments. Using the word *locked* rather than some conventional word like *visible* is an economical way of projecting the exact description. And "*the cars that hissed by*" conveys what cars sound like on wet pavement.

I have always wanted to throw this particular description in the faces of the critics who attack Spillane, because it reveals real literary talent. Unfortunately, he does not always live up to it; he has some sloppy passages in his writing. But you judge a person's literary talent as you judge his intelligence: by what he has demonstrated as his best potential. If he can do *this*, he could bring all of his writing up to the same standard.

In the next paragraph, "*burying my head in the collar of my raincoat, with the night pulled in around me like a blanket*" is again a colorful description. Spillane names the essentials and gives the reader a feel of what it is like to walk with a raised collar on a foggy night.

The next sentence is the best: "*I walked and I smoked and I flipped the spent butts ahead of me and watched them arch to the pavement and fizzle out with one last wink.*" This accomplishes two things: it indicates the character of the man walking and it conveys the exact description. The phrase "*arch to the pavement*" achieves its effect through great economy and precision. Spillane could have said that the butts "fell in an arched line" or merely "fell"; instead, he selects one verb that describes exactly *how* they fell (it is a slightly manufactured verb, but legitimate in the context). And the "*last wink*" is his best touch: that one last spark sets the mood of the whole scene.

From this point on, Spillane lets his standard slip.

"*If there was life behind the windows of the buildings on either side of me, I didn't notice it.*" Although adequate, this is an easier, less distinguished way of describing something.

What is very bad is the grammatical error of saying "*why I wanted it so nice and all alone*." The colloquial style is proper, particularly in a story written in the first person; but it is not proper to use colloquialism in the form of crude grammar.

For instance, the sentence "*I walked and I smoked and I flipped the spent butts*" is colloquial, yet of high literary quality; it is said simply, in a tone which this type of character would use, but there is great artistic care behind it. By contrast, "*why I wanted it so nice and all alone*" is not a clear sentence. It is the kind of sentence a writer might get away with by his tone of voice if he is dictating, but it does not work on paper. It is off-focus; one sort of knows what it means, but only sort of; and after the precision and economy of the preceding, it is particularly out of key.

Such carelessness in combination with the better writing is unfortunately characteristic of Spillane. The lesson is: No matter how much talent you have, if you let your focus slip on any sentence or paragraph, it will show in a slacking of your workmanship. So focus equally on every part of your writing, whether it is the key paragraph or the little transition paragraph. Not all of them have to be equally brilliant or significant, but they all have to be written with the same care.

From *The Web and the Rock* by Thomas Wolfe

That hour, that moment, and that place struck with a peerless coincision upon the very heart of his own youth, the crest and zenith of his own desire. The city had never seemed as beautiful as it looked that night. For the first time he saw that New York was supremely, among the cities of the world, the city of the night. There had been achieved here a loveliness that was astounding and incomparable, a kind of modern beauty, inherent to its place and time, that no other place nor time could match. He realized suddenly that the beauty of other cities of the night—of Paris spread below one from the butte of Sacré Cœur, in its vast, mysterious geography of lights, fumed here and there by drowsy, sensual, and mysterious blossoms of nocturnal radiance; of London with its smoky nimbus of fogged light, which was so peculiarly thrilling because it was so vast, so lost in the illimitable—had each its special quality, so lovely and mysterious, but had yet produced no beauty that could equal this.

The city blazed there in his vision in the frame of night, and for the first time his vision phrased it as it had never done before. It was a cruel city, but it was a lovely one; a savage city, yet it had such tenderness; a bitter, harsh, and violent catacomb of stone and steel and tunneled rock, slashed savagely with light, and roaring, fighting a constant ceaseless warfare of men and of machinery; and yet it was so sweetly and so delicately pulsed, as full of warmth, of passion, and of love, as it was full of hate.

This is as subjective a description as one could put on paper: it is all estimates, and the reader is never told *what* the author is estimating.

Imagine that Wolfe is talking about a view not of a city, but of a plain at night. "The plains of New Jersey were incomparable to the plains of Brittany or Normandy." He could use the same description, with the same adjectives and emotions, since the reader is never told why he is saying any of these things. Wolfe does not offer a single concrete to differentiate New York from anything else.

The author here cannot distinguish between object and subject, between the sight of New York and what that sight makes him feel. He projects his feeling as if it were a description of the city—as if he has said something about New York by saying that New York makes him feel that it is lovely. But this "lovely" is an estimate based on something. He has not told the reader what.

When one examines the particular things he states, there is a whole series of unanswered whys.

"*The city had never seemed as beautiful as it looked that night.*" He never says why. "*For the first time he saw that New York was supremely, among the cities of the world, the city of the night.*" He does not say why, or what a city of the night is, as distinguished from a city of the day. "*There had been achieved here a loveliness that was astounding and incomparable*"—why?—"*a kind of modern beauty, inherent to its place and time, that no other place nor time could match.*" What is "modern beauty"? "*He realized suddenly that the beauty of other cities of the night*"—why are Paris and London cities of the night?—"*had each its special quality, so lovely and mysterious.*" He does not say *what* special qualities, or what is lovely and mysterious about them. Instead, he gives the reader two interchangeable generalities about Paris and London: "*vast, mysterious geography of lights, fumed here and there by drowsy, sensual, and mysterious blossoms of nocturnal radiance*" and "*smoky nimbus of fogged light, which was so peculiarly thrilling because it was so vast, so lost in the illimitable.*" Is there any specific difference between the two? None.

One can guess from the names of New York, Paris, and London, and from the words "*modern beauty*," that Wolfe saw some difference between a city of skyscrapers and cities of older monuments. Had he contrasted the lights and angular structures of skyscrapers to ancient domes and the spires of churches, this would have given meaning to what he is implying. He must have seen *something* that made him call one city modern and the others not, and also some difference between Paris and London. But he did not identify it even to himself, let alone to the reader. All he focused on was that the three sights made him feel differently.

One cannot convey an emotion as such; one can convey it only through that which produced it, or through a conclusion drawn from the emotion. Here the author does try to project an emotion as such—and what is the result? "*Blossoms of nocturnal radiance,*" which is neither emotion, thought, nor description, but merely words.

Now observe the words "*Paris spread below one from the butte of Sacré Cœur.*" Given the absence of any specific description, this reference presupposes that the reader has been to Paris, stood on this elevation, and seen this sight. To expect that kind of knowledge from the reader is to step outside the confines of objectivity; the reader has to learn the concretes of the story from what the author writes. This kind of reference actually implies: "I'm a cosmopolitan traveler and I know the sight, and if you local yokels don't, that's your fault." I doubt that this was Wolfe's intention, but such is always the implication of any dropping of foreign or scientific allusions which presuppose special knowledge on the reader's part.

Do not mention any landmark unless you describe it for the benefit of the uninitiated; otherwise, it is merely a label stuck on your luggage to impress your friends. Even if you write about New York, do not merely say "the Empire State Building rising above the skyline." For the benefit of those who have not seen New York, give a brief description first of the shape of the Empire State Building. If you then want to use the actual name, it will be proper. But it is never proper merely to sling names.

Now observe, in the second paragraph, a peculiar sentence which supports my statement that Wolfe does not distinguish between object and subject: "*The city blazed there in his vision in the frame of night, and for the first time his vision phrased it as it had never done before.*" A vision cannot phrase anything. Wolfe believes that his *vision* is providing him with all his estimates—that the mere sight of a city can tell him that the city is cruel and lovely, full of love and of hate. That is not possible.

What is missing here is why and how he saw all of this. He should have given a specific description to make the reader conclude that it is a cruel, savage city, etc.—if this estimate is based on Wolfe's vision of this particular night. Or, if the estimate is based on memory or on his knowledge of the city, he should similarly have shown why he was drawn to make the estimate at this time and in connection with this view.

The following description is too wide: "*a bitter, harsh, and violent catacomb of stone and steel and tunneled rock, slashed savagely with light.*" To say about something that "it's stone, steel, and tunneled rock" might be an effective summary if some particulars are given. Left by itself, it is too easy, by which I mean "too generalized."

The last of this sentence is ridiculous: "*it was so sweetly and so delicately pulsed*"—if by "pulse" he means the noise or vibrations, what can be sweet or delicate about the pulse of a city?—"*as full of warmth, of passion, and of love, as it was full of hate.*" This sounds like a bad politician slinging immense generalities with no content.

This whole passage is the archetype of floating abstractions, and of a description which describes nothing.

Naturalistic Description

The essence of Naturalistic description is cataloguing. Take the description of a doctor's office in the first chapter of Sinclair Lewis's *Arrowsmith*, particularly the following description of the doctor's sink:

"The most unsanitary corner was devoted to the cast-iron sink, which was oftener used for washing eggy breakfast plates than for sterilizing instruments. On its ledge were a broken test-tube, a broken fishhook, an unlabeled and forgotten bottle of pills, a nail-bristling heel, a frayed cigar-butt, and a rusty lancet stuck in a potato."

This catalogue would give one a clear description if one were a mover and had to pack those things. But it does not jell into an overall impression of what kind of place the office was.

In *Dodsworth*, Lewis has an account of Dodsworth's impression of an English train:

"And the strangeness of having framed pictures of scenery behind the seats; of having hand straps—the embroidered silk covering so rough to the finger-tips, the leather inside so smooth and cool—beside the doors. And the greater strangeness of admitting that these seats were more comfortable than the flinty Pullman chairs of America."

These are observant concretes of the kind a returning traveler would tell his friends about. But they are not an artistic description of the *essence* of an English train compartment.

A Naturalistic writer may sometimes have a good description. Tolstoy, the archetype of a Naturalist, often has very eloquent ones. But to the extent to which they are good, they are done by the Romantic method—i.e., by means of carefully selected, well-observed concretes that capture the essentials of a scene.

Analysis of "A Letter on Style" by Sinclair Lewis

I suspect that no competent and adequately trained writer ever, after his apprenticeship, uses the word "style" in regard to his own work. If he did, he would become so self-conscious that he would be quite unable to write. He may—if I myself am normal he certainly does—consider specific problems of "style." He may say, "That sentence hasn't the right swing," or "That speech is too highfalutin' for a plain chap like this character," or "That sentence is banal—got it from that idiotic editorial I was reading yesterday." The generic concept of "style," as something apart from, distinguishable from, the matter, the thought, the story, does not come to his mind.

He writes as God lets him. He writes—if he is good enough!—as Tilden plays tennis or as Dempsey fights, which is to say, he throws himself into it with never a moment of the dilettante's sitting back and watching himself perform.

This whole question of style vs. matter, of elegant style vs. vulgar, of simplicity vs. embroidering, is as metaphysical and vain as the outmoded (and I suspect the word "outmoded" is a signal of "bad style") discussions of Body and Soul and Mind. Of such metaphysics, we have had enough. Today, east and north of Kansas City, Kansas, we do not writhe in such fantasies. We cannot see that there is any distinction between Soul and Mind. And we believe that we know that with a sick Soul-Mind, we shall have a sick Body; and that with a sick Body, the Mind-Soul cannot be sane. And, still more, we are weary of even such a clarification of that metaphysics. We do not, mostly, talk of Body generically, but say, prosaically, "My liver's bad and so I feel cross."

So is it with that outworn conception called "style."

"Style" is the manner in which a person expresses what he feels. It is dependent on two things: his ability to feel, and his possession, through reading or conversation, of a vocabulary adequate to express his feeling. Without adequate feeling, which is a quality not to be learned in schools, and without vocabulary, which is a treasure less to be derived from exterior instruction than from the inexplicable qualities of memory and good taste, he will have no style.

There is probably more nonsense written regarding the anatomy of "style" than even the anatomies of virtue, sound government, and love. Instruction in "style," like instruction in every other aspect of education, cannot be given to anyone who does not instinctively know it at the beginning.

This is good style:

John Smith meets James Brown on Main Street, Sauk Centre, Minnesota, and remarks, "Mornin'! Nice day!" It is not merely good style; it is perfect. Were he to say, "Hey, youse," or were he to say, "My dear neighbor, it refreshes the soul to encounter you this daedal morn, when from yon hill the early sun its beams displays," he would equally have bad style.

And this is good style: In *The Principles and Practice of Medicine* by Osler and McCrae, it stands:

"Apart from dysentery of the Shiga type, the amoebic and terminal forms, there is a variety of ulcerative colitis, sometimes of great severity, not uncommon in England and the United States."

And this to come is also good style, no better than the preceding and no worse, since each of them completely expresses its thought:

> *A savage place! as holy and enchanted*
> *As e'er beneath a waning moon was haunted*
> *By woman wailing for her demon-lover!*

That I should write ever as absolutely as Coleridge, as Osler and McCrae, or as Jack Smith at ease with Jim Brown, seems to me improbable. But at least I hope that, like them, I shall ever be so absorbed in what I have to say that I shall, like them, write without for one moment stopping to say, "Is this good style?"*

When Lewis says that no competent writer uses the word *style* in regard to his own work, he means that a writer cannot think of a style when he works. This is proper advice; you must not aim self-consciously at a style while you are expressing a thought. But it does not follow, as Lewis implies, that a writer cannot ever hold in his mind a concept of style—that he cannot ever think of style, or judge his own writing, or hold literary standards.

Lewis says that a writer may "consider specific problems of 'style.' " He may say, "That sentence hasn't the right swing," or "That speech is too highfalutin'," or "That sentence is banal." Lewis knows that these

*"A Letter on Style" (1932), reprinted in H. E. Maule and M. H. Cane, eds., *The Man from Main Street* (New York: Random House, 1953).

concretes pertain to style. Why then does he refuse to recognize the general abstraction that unites them? He in effect says: "I just work by rule of thumb. I somehow know when a sentence hasn't the right swing or when another sentence is banal; but I must not call it 'style.' " Why not?

The antiabstraction premise of his article is typical of a Naturalist. A Naturalist is concerned with concrete details and is reluctant ever to explain a wider "why." There are, he holds, no wider "whys." Observe Lewis's defiant, almost angry tone when he denies the necessity of being concerned with broad abstractions. He clearly had certain valid stylistic habits, which he could identify, but was militantly reluctant to do any further thinking or identification. (His antiabstraction approach is one reason why he was often guilty of sloppy writing, and why he was never fully satisfied with his own work.)

Lewis makes it appear that style is something precious, something too "literary," and that he is simply throwing out an old-fashioned word—when he is in fact throwing out the whole abstraction of style, and all abstract standards of writing. The author of *Babbitt*, the archsatirist of the mediocre and vulgar, talks in this article like a Babbitt.

He says that a writer writes "as God lets him." He was not religious, so this is a humorous line—but what does it imply? That we do not know where writing comes from. He says that a writer writes "as Tilden plays tennis or as Dempsey fights, which is to say, he throws himself into it with never a moment of the dilettante's sitting back and watching himself perform." If you are critical of your own work—not in the process of writing, but before and after—that is not the sign of the dilettante; it is the sign of the professional. Tilden and Dempsey had to do an enormous amount of studying and practice before they could throw themselves into a match without any thought about their technique. The comparison is valid: you have to do all your practice and studying beforehand. But you cannot throw yourself into a ring, or a story, without thinking about it and simply act "as God lets you." It was not God that made Dempsey a prizefighter.

Lewis says: " 'Style' is the manner in which a person expresses what he feels. It is dependent on two things: his ability to feel, and his possession, through reading or conversation, of a vocabulary adequate to express his feeling." Observe that he does not mention thinking; to him, *feeling* is a primary. "Without adequate feeling, which is a quality not to be learned in schools, and without vocabulary, which is a treasure less to be derived from exterior instruction than from the *inexplicable* qualities of memory and good taste, [a writer] will have no style" (emphasis added). According to Lewis, feelings are inexplicable; so is good taste; so is memory; so is the acquisition of a vocabulary.

"Instruction in 'style,' " Lewis says, "like instruction in every other aspect of education, cannot be given to anyone who does not instinctively know it at the beginning." Again, he assumes that one's capacity for any subject is innate and therefore cannot be acquired or taught. If a young writer went by this advice, he would be entering a career as a horse race, on a blind guess: "Do I have talent? Do I have memory? Do I have good taste?"—with none of these things to be explained or acquired.

All the things Lewis takes as inexplicable and irreducible primaries are in fact explicable and acquirable. Your ability to feel is a function of your ability to think, and thinking is volitional and can be learned. Your taste depends on your premises. Memory is a function of valuing; the hardest thing on earth is to remember something that is of no importance to you—for instance, forcing yourself to memorize by automatic rote. And you acquire a vocabulary simply by being convinced of the importance of words, so that you pay attention to their shadings when you read or speak.

When Lewis gives examples of good style, he says that these are good because each sentence completely expresses its thought. This is correct; as I put it, good style is form following function.

Clarity, however, is not the only important attribute of style. What constitutes the heart of any style is the clarity of the thoughts a writer expresses—plus the *kind* of thoughts he chooses to express. In the lines Lewis quotes from Coleridge, a vastly greater amount of information—of thought, emotion, connotation—is conveyed than in his medical quotation or in the "John Smith meets James Brown" sentence. For a textbook, a legal document, or a synopsis, Lewis's medical quotation is good style; for fiction, the same style would be miserable—not because it is not clear, but because too little is said. With the same amount of words, a fiction writer can say much more.

A good style is one that conveys the most with the greatest economy of words. In a textbook, the ideal is to communicate one line of thought or set of facts as clearly as possible. For a literary style, much more is necessary. A great literary style is one that combines five or more different meanings in one clear sentence (I do not mean ambiguity but the communication of different issues).

Observe how many issues I cover in any one sentence in *Atlas Shrugged*, and on how many levels. In this context, I want to repeat an eloquent compliment that Alan Greenspan once gave me: he said that I do with words what Rachmaninoff does with music. Rachmaninoff's compositions are complex; he combines so many elements in his music that one has to stretch one's mind to hear them all at once. I always try to do the same in writing. (I am not here comparing degrees of talent, but merely pointing out the principle.)

I never waste a sentence on saying: "John Smith meets James Brown." That is too easy; it is playing the piano with one finger. Say much more, just as clearly—say it in chords, with a whole orchestration. That is good style.

10

Particular Issues of Style

Narrative versus Dramatization

I use the word *narrative* in two senses. From the standpoint of *form*, narrative is that which is not dialogue; everything said by the author, as opposed to the characters, is narrative (including the "he said" and "she said in a trembling voice" between the dialogue lines). From the standpoint of *structure*, however, narrative is that which is not dramatized.

To *dramatize* something is to show it as if it were happening before the reader's eyes, so that he is in the position of an observer at the scene. To *narrate*, by contrast, is to synopsize: you tell the reader about something which has happened, but you do not let him be a witness. This is a legitimate device; in fact, you could not write a novel without using narrative. If a story were presented exclusively in terms of dramatic action, it would be a play.

A silent action—an escape, say, from a burning building, with no dialogue—is dramatized if it is described in detail. Predominantly, however, the dramatized scenes of a novel are those in which dialogue is reproduced.

Conversely, dialogue usually occurs only in dramatized scenes, but there are exceptions. When you synopsize a conversation in narrative, you can quote a single sentence to feature the essence of the conversation, or to sharpen some salient point. A whole exchange of dialogue—four or more lines—constitutes a dramatized scene. But the quotation, for emphasis, of just one line of dialogue in a narrative passage does not make the passage a dramatization.

When is it proper to narrate and when to dramatize an event? There can be as many variations as there are stories, but the one rule is: *Always dramatize important events.*

Dramatization serves as the emphasis of your story. The key events should be dramatized. The less important material, such as transitions, can be narrated.

The beginning of the chapter "Account Overdrawn" in *Atlas Shrugged* is a montage of the progressive economic destruction of the country. In order to make the description colorful, I give semi-dramatization to particular details, but the overall passage is merely a narrative of what happens during that winter to the whole country. Then I come to the meeting where the board of directors decide to close the John Galt Line. That is dramatized. In the preceding months, no event was important enough to focus the story on. But the closing of the John Galt Line is an important point in the story; therefore, I dramatize it—I reproduce the dialogue so that you, the reader, are present at that meeting.

Many nineteenth-century novels, such as *Quo Vadis* and *The Scarlet Letter*, are written too much in straight narrative. (This is a minor flaw compared to the literary values of these two works.) One good aspect of the old silent movie of *The Scarlet Letter*, starring Lillian Gish, was that it dramatized (in most cases quite well) important events that in the novel are merely told about.

You must be careful and skillful when you combine dramatization and narrative.

Sometimes an author presents a scene in detail, the dialogue is reproduced verbatim, and then there is a paragraph saying: "They argued in this manner late into the night, but reached no conclusion." This is switching from dramatization to narrative, summing up the ending of a scene in narrative form. Sometimes an author begins with detailed dialogue, then switches to narrative, then goes *back* to the dramatized scene. All of this is legitimate—but be careful of your balance. Be sure to narrate only that which is unimportant. In other words, be sure that your highlights are dramatized.

Do not start a scene in dialogue and then cover something more crucial in narrative. Suppose you reproduce the opening dialogue of a marital quarrel and then you say: "They argued into the night, and finally she declared that she would leave him." This is bad writing. I do not mean that there is a rule about never narrating a quarrel or a decision; it can be narrated if it is only an incidental development in the progress of the story. But if you stop on a scene at all, if you bring the reader in to witness it, do not cheat him of the scene's climax.

There is another danger I want to warn you against.

I once read a story by a beginner in which a father comes back from Europe to his wife and little son after a long absence. The narrative says: "The boy was fascinated by the sophisticated, cosmopolitan conversation of his father." Then the dialogue says: " 'The English sure have a wonderful way of cooking beef,' said the father. 'Yes,' said the mother, 'but on the other hand, I hear that the French restaurants are pretty good.' 'Well, I wouldn't say so,' answered the father. 'The French go more for sauces and trimmings, but for real beefsteak, give me English cooking.' "

In the same category are the many stories, usually about a poet, where the author spends a lot of time in narrative telling the reader what a genius that poet is—and then he gives some samples which are dreadful.

Never declare in narrative the opposite of what you illustrate in action or dialogue. Whenever you make estimates in narrative—whenever you announce that your character is brave or a genius or good or noble—be sure that the action and dialogue support your estimate. If you say that a man's conversation is sophisticated—show it. Otherwise, do not make the estimate.

In general, it is inadvisable to make such estimates—and you can never count primarily on your narrative to convey characterization. To show a man of genius, you have to show by his actions and words that that is what he is; to show a brave man, you have to give him some actions displaying courage. But there *are* instances where it is necessary to summarize something in narrative. If so, be sure that what is dramatized supports your estimate. The principle here is that of assertion versus proof. Do not assert anything which you cannot prove.

Exposition

Exposition is the communication of knowledge which the reader requires in order to understand a scene. At the start of a story, it is the communication of what has happened before the start. You can also have exposition *during* a story. After a time lapse, for instance, the reader might need to know what has happened in the preceding year.

The one rule about exposition is: *Do not let it show*. Exposition is like the seams in clothing: in a well-made garment, the seams are not glaring at you; they are skillfully hidden, yet they hold the garment together.

By "Do not let your exposition show," I mean: Do not devote any action or line merely to explaining something. Make the exposition part of some statement which has a different point—a point necessary for the progress of the scene.

For instance, do not have two characters talk about something that they both know. It is bad exposition to have a businessman say to his partner: "As you well know, our bills are long overdue." Instead, have him give instructions to his new secretary about a letter to the bank, telling her: "We are in a hurry because our bills are overdue."

Whenever one character communicates something in dialogue to another, there must be a reason why the second character has to be told the information—a reason related to the action of the scene. The communication should be part of some purpose with which the scene is concerned, and all the necessary information should be conveyed in the discussion of that purpose.

The best example of this in my own work is the scene between James Taggart and Eddie Willers in the first chapter of *Atlas Shrugged*, where Eddie is urging Taggart to do something about their Colorado branch line and Taggart is evading. If you read that scene, you will be surprised to see how much you are learning—under the guise of their argument—about the overall situation of Taggart Transcontinental.

An example of bad exposition is the kind of old-fashioned play which opens with two servants talking onstage: " 'The master is away.' 'The pearls are in the safe.' 'The mistress is entertaining a suspicious character on the veranda.' " Shortly thereafter, the pearls are stolen.

Devoting a line to explaining something is sometimes proper. An example is the exposition right after the names of the various intellectuals at the party at Rearden's in *Atlas Shrugged*.

"Bertram Scudder stood slouched against the bar. His long, thin face looked as if it had shrunk inward, with the exception of his mouth and eyeballs, which were left to protrude as three soft globes. He was the editor of a magazine called *The Future* and he had written an article on Hank Rearden, entitled 'The Octopus.' "

This is a proper use of exposition since it is done in the nature of a parenthesis, without stopping the action.

If you have a complex exposition to give, you will in the beginning be anxious to give it all at once. It will seem to you that you have to tell the reader everything or he will not understand you. Do not be fooled by this; the story will carry if you make just one point clear. A few sentences later, you divulge something else, and so on. Feed one bit of information at a time.

There are no rules about where to feed information or at what tempo; you have to gauge this by the general structure of your story. Some of the information conveyed in the scene between Eddie Willers and James Taggart I could have planted in advance, by having Eddie worry about the Colorado branch line, or stop outside Taggart's office to discuss something with an underling. But since I *could* impart all the necessary information in the major scene, it was better to do so than to give the exposition special emphasis. Also, I had already planted enough ominous overtones to convey that something is going on which disturbs Eddie. I would have weakened the drama had I given the reader any inkling of the specifics until he sees them in action, in the form of a conflict.

The ingenuity you can exhibit in regard to exposition is unlimited. You can make an advantage out of a liability: instead of being burdened with your exposition, you can feed it at the points where it fits the narrative or the dialogue and makes the scene more dramatic.

But be careful to be objective. Do not rely on any knowledge which the reader does not yet have. You might deliberately make two characters talk for a while in a mysterious way until you clarify what they are talking about; that is legitimate. But watch for when you have held the mystery—or withheld the information—for too long. Instead of being intriguing, a scene that is bewildering for too long becomes boring.

Flashbacks

A flashback is a scene taken from the past. It is a dramatized exposition.

The story of Dagny and Francisco's childhood in *Atlas Shrugged* is an example. Since their relationship in the novel is based on what happened in their childhood, I want the reader to know about this before he meets Francisco as a character. Had I merely summarized their childhood in a paragraph, that would have been exposition. But since I wanted to cover their childhood in detail, I literally had to go back into the past, and that is a flashback.

The only standard for when to use flashbacks is the importance of the information you want to convey. Incidental information you cover in narrative. If the information is important to the story, it is better to go into a detailed flashback.

But do not burden a story with unnecessary flashbacks. If in every other chapter you go into a flashback, you confuse the reader. Some writers have flashbacks within flashbacks: they start with a middle-aged person in the present, then show a flashback from his youth, during which they show a flashback from his childhood, then come back to the youth, then to the present. This can be gotten away with, but it is not advisable.

There is no rule that limits the length of a flashback in proportion to the rest of the story. Suppose that the events of a story span several years and come to a conclusion in one last meeting between two characters. In order to focus that meeting, the author might first establish in a few lines the fact that these characters are about to meet; then, in a long flashback, present everything that happened in the past; and then, coming back to the present and the meeting, describe the conclusion in a final few lines. While reading the flashback, the reader waits for the story to reach the present again, anticipating that something will happen at the promised meeting between the two characters. And since the proper focus has been established from the outset, the final lines come across much more forcefully than they would have done had the story been told in chronological order.

The suspense and heightened interest of such a structure depends on the reader's unspoken assumption that the writer is rational and has a reason for constructing his story this way. By contrast, a modern writer would start a story as described above and never come back to the present; or he would come back, but then nothing significant would happen.

It is legitimate now and then to remind the reader of the present during a long flashback—but only if you have a reason for it and you advance the story by that means.

The only rule for going into a flashback is to avoid confusing the reader. Mark clearly when you go from the present to the past and when you go back to the present again. The simplest way is to say: "He remembered the time when . . ." or "He thought of the days of his childhood." This is not bromidic, because it is direct. But there are more interesting ways of doing it.

One of my best flashback transitions is the one to Dagny and Francisco's childhood. She is walking to his hotel, and yet she is thinking that she should be running:

"She wondered why she felt that she wanted to run, that she should be running; no, not down this street; down a green hillside in the blazing sun to the road on the edge of the Hudson, at the foot of the Taggart estate. That was the way she always ran when Eddie yelled, 'It's Frisco d'Anconia!' and they both flew down the hill to the car approaching on the road below."

Although the reader notices the transition, it comes naturally.

Now consider the scene in *Atlas Shrugged* where James Taggart spills water on the table before Cherryl starts thinking about the events of the past year.

" 'Oh, for Christ's sake!' he screamed, smashing his fist down on the table. 'Where have you been all these years? What sort of world do you think you're living in?' His blow had upset his water glass and the water went spreading in dark stains over the lace of the tablecloth."

I do not have Cherryl go into the past by means of the spilled water, but I use it later to bring her back to the present:

"What do you want of me?—she asked, looking at the whole long torture of her marriage that had not lasted the full span of one year.

" 'What do you want of me?' she asked aloud—and saw that she was sitting at the table in her dining room, looking at Jim, at his feverish face, and at a drying stain of water on the table."

I planted the spilled water early in the scene in order to mention it later, as a touch pertaining to this particular dining room at this moment. Recognizing it as such, the reader knows that Cherryl is now back at dinner with James, where she was before she started thinking of the past. Had I not used the water, or some equivalent device, it would not have been clear that Cherryl is now back in the present; it might have seemed as if I were describing some other scene of the past year.

A tricky transition is good when it is warranted by the material, so that it appears natural; but avoid artificial tricks that are planted only for the purpose of the transition. For instance, the spilled water in the above scene is legitimate because it serves another purpose: to illustrate James's bad temper and violence. Had I written a scene between a calm, polite, happy couple, and suddenly, by sheer accident, the man spilled water because I later needed it as a signpost, that would have been artificial.

Transitions

A difficult problem that one usually does not think of until one comes up against it is how to take the action from one point to another—for instance, how to take a person out of a room and down to the street, or have him cross a room to pick up something on the other side. On the stage, those small movements are taken care of unobtrusively by the director, who has to plan them so that they *are* unobtrusive. In a novel, they are the writer's responsibility.

When you write a scene, you must preserve the reality of the setting. For instance, you have said that the heroine is by the fireplace to the left of the room and that some document is on a table to the right, and now she has to cross the room and seize the document. If you do not mention that she walks across the room, the reader will notice an inconsistency in the scene. But to mention it might be a bad interruption.

When you do not want to interrupt a scene with a technical reminder like that, "think outside the square." Do not limit yourself to the dry assignment of saying, like a stage direction: "She crosses to the table." Instead of saying "She rushed across the room and seized the document," say something like "Her dress swished with the speed of her steps as she rushed across the room and seized the document." Then the purpose of the sentence appears to be the description of the movement, which might tie in with the emotional violence of the scene (or whatever the mood is). But you have covered the point of taking the heroine to the other side.

In other words, when you need a "stage indication," always tie it to some element of the scene—any element other than the dry factual reminder. As with exposition, you bring in a transition when your focus is on something else pertaining to the scene.

Suppose you finish a scene played in a house and you have to take the heroine outside. You need to give the reader some sense of transition, but you do not want to describe the heroine going down the stairs. So start the next paragraph with "The street looked lonely and deserted as she emerged from the house."

The following is an example from the first chapter of *Atlas Shrugged*. Dagny, who has fallen asleep on a train, awakens and asks a passenger: "How long have we been standing?" Then:

"The man looked after her, sleepily astonished, because she leaped to her feet and rushed to the door.

"There was a cold wind outside, and an empty stretch of land under an empty sky. She heard weeds rustling in the darkness. Far ahead, she saw the figures of men standing by the engine—and above them, hanging detached in the sky, the red light of a signal."

She is out already. I did not cover the technicalities of her opening the door and rushing down the steps; I switched viewpoint.

Do not say: "Six months later." Instead, present your characters swimming at the beach, and at the beginning of the next scene, say: "It was snowing heavily."

There are other such devices, but the principle is always: Don't let your seams show. You cover the seams by connecting them to some other pertinent aspect of the scene. Do not, however, make your transitions so indirect that the result is awkward and forced. Then the seams will show more than ever.

Metaphors

The purpose of metaphors, or comparisons, is epistemological. If I describe a spread of snow and I say, "The snow was white like sugar," the comparison conveys a sensory focus on the whiteness of the snow. It is more colorful than merely saying "The snow was white." If I describe sugar, I can do it in reverse: "The sugar in the bowl was white like snow." This conveys a better impression of the sugar than if I merely said: "The sugar was white."

The operative principle here is that of *abstraction*. If you describe only one object, in concrete terms, it is difficult to convey a sensuous impression: you *tell* about the object, but you do not *show* it. The introduction of another concrete with the same attribute makes the two together give a clear sensuous image—it isolates the attribute by making the reader's mind form an abstraction. The reader's lightning-like visualization of the whiteness of snow and the whiteness of sugar makes that *whiteness* stand out in his mind as if he had seen it.

When you select a comparison, you must consider not only the exact attribute you want to feature, but also the *connotations* that will be raised in the reader's mind. For instance, the old bromide "Her lips were like ripe cherries" was not bad when said the first time. Cherries connote something red, sensuous, glistening, and attractive. But suppose I said: "Her lips were like ripe tomatoes." Tomatoes are also red and shining, but the comparison sounds ridiculous because the connotations are wrong. Ripe tomatoes make you think of something squashy, of the kitchen, of an unappetizing salad. The things connected with the concept of a vegetable are not romantic.

If you want something to sound attractive, be sure to make your comparison glamorous and attractive. If you want to destroy something, do the opposite.

An example of the latter is the undignified comparison in my description of Ellsworth Toohey in *The Fountainhead*: his ears "flared out in solitary nakedness, like the handles of a bouillon cup." It would be bad writing to say "His ears stuck out like wings," because the attribute described is unattractive, but a comparison to wings suggests something soaring and attractive. To bring connotations of something good into a derogatory description is the opposite mistake of comparing the lips of a beautiful woman to ripe tomatoes.

It is by means of the connotations of your comparisons that you can do the best objective slanted writing. By "objective," I mean that the reader's mind draws the conclusion—it is not you, the writer, who calls his attention to the fact that a certain person is ugly or undignified. To be objective, you have to *show*, not tell. You do it by selecting the connotations of your comparisons.

You can do the same with simple adjectives, which have definite connotations or shades of meaning. "The man was tall and slender" is an attractive description, whereas "He was tall, lanky, and gawky" is not. In description by means of comparisons, the field of selection is much wider, but the identical principle applies. You can describe the same quality as attractive or not according to what metaphors you use.

As a smaller matter, do not overload a paragraph with metaphors. Instead of making the description more colorful, this blunts the perception of the reader. He is lost among so many concretes out of different categories that they cease to work on him, and he has no impression left in his mind. It is like showing too many pictures too fast.

Above all, avoid two metaphors to describe the same thing. Sometimes, two clever images might occur to you to describe an object. You have to be ruthless and select the one you think is better. A repetition is always weakening; it has the effect of projecting the author's doubt, his uncertainty that the first description is good enough.

Descriptions

I describe my characters at their first appearance. Since I want the reader to perceive the scene as if he were there, I indicate as soon as possible what the characters look like.

Sometimes I depart from this deliberately. In *Atlas Shrugged*, Wesley Mouch is not described in his introductory scene; I give him a few insipid lines and nothing more. The next time he is mentioned, as the new economic dictator of the country, I cash in on the fact that the reader, if he remembers him at all, remembers a total nonentity.

But my heroes and heroines I always describe at their introduction.

I decide how long a description should be by the nature of the buildup—by how much significance the context has prepared the reader to attach to a character.

In *Atlas Shrugged*, I prepare James Taggart's description in the following manner. Eddie Willers has been thinking about the oak tree in his childhood and about his shock upon discovering that it was only the shell of its former strength. Then he comes to the Taggart building, and I describe that he feels the same about this building as he used to feel about the oak. And then he walks into the heart of the building, into the office of the president:

"James Taggart sat at his desk. He looked like a man approaching fifty, who had crossed into age from adolescence, without the intermediate stage of youth. He had a small, petulant mouth, and thin hair clinging to a bald forehead. His posture had a limp, decentralized sloppiness, as if in defiance of his tall, slender body, a body with an elegance of line intended for the confident poise of an aristocrat, but transformed into the gawkiness of a lout. The flesh of his face was pale and soft. His eyes were pale and veiled, with a glance that moved slowly, never quite stopping, gliding off and past things in eternal resentment of their existence. He looked obstinate and drained. He was thirty-nine years old."

I have warned the reader that Eddie Willers is inclined to rely on strength long after it is gone, and that he thinks of the Taggart building as a powerful oak. Then I tell the reader about the gray dust at the heart of *this* oak.

Because of the buildup, the reader is willing to read the description without impatience. Also, when he meets the president of a big railroad and sees a neurotic nonentity, this has some significance. If the president were a conventional man, one could not pause on a long description. But when an obviously vicious man is in charge of an organization that has just been built up as very impressive, a lengthy description is warranted.

My longest description of a character in any of my novels is that of John Galt at the beginning of Part III of *Atlas Shrugged*. Having spent two parts of the book hearing about this man—and having just seen the heroine crash in an airplane, pursuing him—the reader is willing to read in detail what he looks like (provided the description makes it worthwhile).

When I introduce minor characters, I usually give them a single line naming something that is characteristic of the type, like "a woman who had large diamond earrings" or "a portly man who wore a green muffler." By implying that one brief characteristic is all that is noteworthy about the person, I establish his unimportance. These lesser types you must not pause on for long.

I recently reread *Ivanhoe*, which I had not read since age twelve. It is a marvelous story, but I mention it here because the first thirteen pages of my edition are devoted to a description of four characters, only one of whom is a principal—and it is not even a description of their faces or personalities, but of their clothes, the harnesses of their horses, and the weapons of their retinues. To include thirteen pages of such descriptions, without any action having yet started and without the reader having been given any reason to be interested in the characters, is very unbalanced.

Never pause on descriptions, whether of characters or locales or anything else, unless you have given the reader reason to be interested.

Dialogue

Even when you select dialogue you think is in style with the class, education, and character of a certain person, your *own* style plays an enormous role.

Sinclair Lewis thinks that a small-town man would say "Mornin'! Nice day!" [see p. 140]. This is Lewis stylizing dialogue in the bad folks-next-door way. If *I* were to project a small-town man, I would have him say "Good morning" (or perhaps even "Hey, you" if it fitted the particular character and relationship).

You do not make an illiterate ruffian talk in abstract, academic terms. But whether you select the kind of vulgar sentences which represent the essential style of his character, or the narrow, local colloquialisms of his day, depends on your own style. (If you compare the illiterate talk of villains or ruffians in a Romantic and a Naturalistic novel, you will see the difference.)

Even in dialogue, your own style rules your selection. Do not give yourself a blank check of this kind: "I'll merely reproduce what I think a character like so-and-so would say." You have to reproduce it in the way your literary premises dictate. Do not attempt to be a Romantic writer, then give your characters Naturalistic dialogue—and, if criticized, say: "Oh, but I heard them talk at Klein's [department store] just like that." You have to reproduce the way women talk at Klein's according to your own style.

I do not mean that you should make all your characters talk in the same way, or talk like yourself. You have to make them talk differently according to their particular characterizations. But the *overall* style and selectivity of the dialogue must be yours.

Slang

If you are writing in the first person and the narrator is supposed to talk colloquially, it is colorful to use slang (the best example is Mickey Spillane). But do not use slang in straight narrative.

There are, however, slang words which are (or are becoming) part of the language, and in those cases you have to exercise your judgment. The slang words that eventually find general acceptance are those for which there is no legitimate equivalent. Some slang words are created precisely to fill a linguistic need. When no respectable English word will give you the exact shade of meaning you want, it is legitimate to use a slang word, provided it has been in circulation for some time and is generally known.

The slang which changes every year is the kind that is used for some purpose other than the communication of meaning. It is always a local affectation—some college or Midwestern expression which is not needed and is repeated strictly because it *is* an affectation. This kind vanishes; a year later, nobody knows what the expression means. Do not use such words unless you are writing some journalistic story of the split second and you intend it to be dead within a year.

The use of slang in dialogue depends on the character speaking. For instance, you can use the word *swanky* in the dialogue of a certain type of person. The word has been used for years and remains in the language. But never use it in narrative, since there is a formal equivalent. (The slang of the split second should not be used even as characterization. It is too perishable and phony.)

Similarly, in regard to swear words and words of insult, you have to judge whether or not a character would speak that kind of language.

Incidentally, there is no word in English to denote a worthless man, except for *bastard. Scoundrel*, *blackguard*, and *rotter* are more British than American; and people never use them; they are antiquated and literary. I think this is one reason why *bastard* became formal English (it is no longer an obscenity and does not involve illegitimate birth, although that is the root of the word). The language did not have a word to express a negative value judgment on a man.

In Russian, I can think of ten or twelve words on the order of the English *bastard*; and there is even more polite usage: words that can be used in a drawing room—all of them expressions of contempt for a man's moral character. This is a significant indication of the opposite metaphysics and morality of the two languages.

The number of words to express human evil is much greater in other languages than in English. For that fact, I give great credit to America.

Obscenities

Do *not* use obscenities—and never mind all the arguments about "realism."

Obscenities are language which implies a value judgment of condemnation or contempt, usually in regard to certain parts of the body and sex. Four-letter words all have non-obscene synonyms; they are obscene not by content, but by their *intention*—the intention being to convey that what is referred to is improper or evil.

Obscene language is based on the metaphysics and morality of the anti-body school of thought. Observe that the more religious a nation is, the more varied and violently obscene is its four-letter-word repertoire. It is said that the Spanish are the most obscene. I do not know Spanish, but I know that Russians have a whole sublanguage—not just single words, but ready-made sentences—all of it concerning sex. (I myself know only a few examples.)

Obscene language is not an objective language which you can use to express your *own* value judgments. It is a language of prefabricated value judgments consisting of the denunciation of sex and this earth and conveying that these are low or damnable. You do not want to subscribe to this premise.

If you write about slum inhabitants or men in the army, you have a difficult literary problem. Modern writers specialize in conveying that men in the army talk in nothing but four-letter words. That I do not believe, but I have heard men of that sort use obscene words under stress. If you have to establish such an atmosphere, a few "darns" or "damns" will not quite do it. It is not, however, necessary to use prefabricated language for the sake of "realism."

The trick is to suggest by the *context* of what is being said that it is abusive or obscene. Do not use the actual terms. Avoid them on the principle by which you would avoid describing horrible operations or ghastly physical illnesses. You may *suggest* these if you want a description of horror—but you do not go into every detail of the color of an infected wound or the maggots on a dead body.

If you are ever tempted to describe something ghastly, ask yourself what your purpose is. If it is to suggest horror, one or two generalized lines will do. It is sufficient to say that someone stumbles upon a half-decomposed corpse; to describe that corpse in every horrible detail is horror for horror's sake. All you will achieve is that your book, no matter what the rest of it consists of, will always connote in the reader's mind that particular touch of horror.

Foreign Words

Do not use foreign words in narrative to show your erudition. Phonies like to stud their conversation with foreign words. If you do that in narrative, you, the author, will sound like a phony.

The same applies to dialogue. If you are characterizing a phony, it is legitimate to have him use foreign words occasionally. I did that with Guy Francon in *The Fountainhead.* But do not insert foreign words in the dialogue of characters if the story is laid in a foreign country, as many bad television and movie writers do. For instance, a story is laid in Germany; the characters are speaking in English, under the assumption that in fact they are speaking in German; and suddenly they utter words like *liebchen* in the middle of an English dialogue which is supposed to be German anyway. This has the same effect as the one achieved for Guy Francon, who would suddenly use French words to show that he could speak French—the effect of the author showing off that he knows a few German words or has just looked them up in the dictionary.

Sometimes a foreign character [who is actually supposed to be speaking in English] might mispronounce words or have a slightly Germanic way of sentence construction. Some foreigners have a characteristic way of talking if they do not know English well. It is legitimate to convey that, provided you devise your own means of doing it, instead of merely using a bromidic shorthand as a substitute for characterization, and provided you present the character's particular grammatical structure, rather than just the mispronunciation.

Journalistic References

By "journalistic references," I mean the names of living authors, political figures, song hits—any proper names which pertain concretely to a given period. The rule is: Do not use anything of this nature more recent than a hundred years. Anything that has survived for a long time becomes an abstraction, but the fame of the moment is too temporary to include in a story which deals with essentials, not with particular details.

It is all right to use Chopin, but not any contemporary composers, artists, or writers. Even if you are convinced that some contemporary writer is going to be immortal, he will in your story project something too much of the moment. Avoid the names of actual restaurants (which modern Naturalists love to use). You do not want to have your big scene laid in the restaurant that closed last week.

Especially bad are references to political issues. Nothing is as old as yesterday's newspaper, and the issues that are big today are barely remembered two years later. Avoid names like "McCarthy," "Hoover," or "Truman." They are included in most modern writing; read it five years later—it is more dated than ladies' fashions.

(If for some reason you do use something of today, explain what it is, rather than rely on the immediate journalistic context in the reader's mind. That will give the reference a certain feeling of distance and abstraction.)

Every writer, including me, has sometimes been guilty of using journalistic references. In *The Fountainhead*, I should not have described the devil as "a corner lout sipping a bottle of Coca-Cola," and I also regret Coty's powder puffs on Toohey's dressing gown:

"Ellsworth Toohey sat spread out on a couch, wearing a dressing gown. . . . The dressing gown was made of silk bearing the trademarked pattern of Coty's face powder, white puffs on an orange background; it looked daring and gay, supremely elegant through sheer silliness."

There was in fact that kind of material on the market. Today, I would rather have invented some perfume company that used not a powder puff, but something else.

In my original manuscript of *The Fountainhead*, I had references to

Nazism and communism, and even to Hitler and Stalin. [Novelist and political writer] Isabel Paterson, to whom I showed the abstract speeches before the book was published, said to me: "Do not use those narrow political terms, because the theme of your book is wider than the politics of the moment. Granted that the book is directed against fascism and communism, you are really writing about collectivism—any past, present, or future form of it. Do not narrow your subject down to the particular figures of the moment."

I had to think this over for two days before I absorbed the idea; I was so used to the other method that it took quite an effort to cut out those journalistic references. But it was one of the most valuable pieces of advice I ever got in regard to writing. Imagine reading *The Fountainhead* today with references to Hitler and Stalin—it would not be the same novel.

You have to be guided by your theme and by how abstract a level you are writing on. In *We the Living*, I had a lot of journalistic references: specific dates, the Lenin-Trotsky split, and so forth. But that novel deals specifically with the politics of a certain period, so there such references were legitimate. When you deal with history, you obviously mention the concretes of the period.

In *Atlas Shrugged*, I hardly mentioned anybody younger than Plato and Aristotle. More recent references were proper in *The Fountainhead* because the fight for modern architecture occurred in a specific historical period. But *Atlas Shrugged* is of no period and therefore had to be kept the most abstract.

11

Special Forms of Literature

Humor

Humor is a metaphysical negation. We regard as funny that which contradicts reality: the incongruous and the grotesque.

Take the crudest example of humor: a dignified gentleman in top hat and tails walks down the street, slips on a banana peel, and falls down in a ludicrous position. Why is this supposed to be amusing? Because of the incongruity: if a dignified man falls down over a stupid object like a banana peel, it establishes him as contradictory to and unfit to deal with reality. That is what one laughs at.

In another bromide of two-reel comedies, a man comes home while his wife is entertaining a lover. Hiding the lover in a closet, the wife then tries to keep her husband from opening it: he wants to hang up his coat and she prevents him, etc. Why is this supposed to be funny? Because you (the audience) and the woman know the truth of the situation. You are in control of reality; the husband is not. That is the essence of humor.

Observe that man is the only being who can laugh. There is no such thing as a laughing animal. Only man has a volitional consciousness, and thus a choice between that which he regards as serious and that which he does not. Only man has the power to identify: This is reality—and this is a contradiction of reality. An animal does not have the concept *contradiction* (or even the concept *reality*, except by implication); it cannot grasp the issue of being volitionally unfit for reality. But a man can find other men ludicrous if they indulge in contradictions. Why? Because they have the choice of being consistent or not. Their contradictions are sometimes tragic; the smaller ones are funny.

What you find funny depends on what you want to negate. It is proper to laugh at evil (the literary form of which is satire) or at the negligible. But to laugh at the good is vicious. If you laugh at any value that suddenly shows feet of clay, such as in the example of the dignified gentleman slipping on a banana peel, you are laughing at the validity of values as such. On the other hand, if a pompous villain walks down the street—a man whose established attributes are not dignity, but pretentiousness and stuffiness—you may properly laugh if he falls down because what is then being negated is a pretense, not an actual value.

Observe that some people have a good-natured sense of humor, and others a malicious one. Good-natured, charming humor is never directed at a value, but always at the undesirable or negligible. It has the result of *confirming* values; if you laugh at the contradictory or pretentious, you are in that act confirming the real or valuable. Malicious humor, by contrast, is always aimed at some value. For instance, when someone laughs at something that is important to you, that is the undercutting of your value.

The best statement of the difference between the two types of humor occurs in *Atlas Shrugged* when Dagny thinks of the opposite ways in which Francisco and Jim laugh: "Francisco seemed to laugh at things because he saw something much greater. Jim laughed as if he wanted to let nothing remain great."

In this context, you can see why one of Ellsworth Toohey's most evil lines in *The Fountainhead* is his advice that "we must be able to laugh at everything, particularly at ourselves." The fact that one hears that line so often is the worst symptom of our nonvalue age. When that line is repeated too often in a society, it is a sign of the collapse of all values.

Observe modern magazines when they do profiles on celebrities whom they support or agree with: they always do it in a snide manner of laughing at the very people they are glamorizing. This style was once reserved for enemies; the press would do a ridiculing article only on someone they disagreed with or wanted to denounce. Today, it is the accepted style for those whom they want to glorify. That is a devastating sign of the policy that says: "Permit nothing to have value."

To say that one does not take something seriously means: "Never mind, it's not important, it doesn't matter one way or another." You can say that only about the things you do not value. If you take *nothing* seriously, it means that you have no values. If you have no values, then the *first* value, the base of all the others—namely, your life—has no value for you.

Let me give a few examples of the two types of humor.

Jean Kerr, the author of *Please Don't Eat the Daisies*, is a benevolent humorist. She is allegedly complaining about the hard lot of a mother and the difficulty of coping with children. For instance, when her children eat the daisies, that is supposed to be a great evil on their part. But is that in fact what she is saying? No; she is really conveying the adventurousness and imagination of her children—their high spirits, which she has such a "hard" time controlling. At one point, when she describes how impossible it is to talk to one of her boys who is very literal-minded, I fell in love with that boy. She tells him to throw all of his clothes into the washing machine, and their conversation then goes something like the following. He says: "All my clothes?" She says: "Yes." "My shoes, too?" "Well, no, not your shoes." "All right, but I'll put in the belt." What comes across from their dialogue is an extremely intelligent, rational child. What Jean Kerr is actually laughing at is the kind of mother who would really consider this bad or difficult. She is negating the difficulty of the situation, and she is glorifying the good qualities of her children.

O. Henry is a benevolent humorist, as is Oscar Wilde in many of his plays, particularly *The Importance of Being Earnest*. *Cyrano de Bergerac* contains a lot of comedy, all of it aimed at destroying the pretentious or the cowardly. Cyrano laughs at villains, not at values or heroes.

Ernst Lubitsch was the only screen director famous for romantic comedies. *Ninotchka*, the Greta Garbo picture he directed, is a good example: it is comedy, but also high romance. What is laughed at is the sordid, undesirable aspects of life—and what comes across *by means of* the humor is the glamour, the romance, and the positive aspects.

In the benevolent type of humor, something good is always involved, as in *Ninotchka*, where the hero and heroine are quite glamorous. *They* are not funny—some of their adventures are; or they are acting humorously toward certain things, but not in a way that undercuts their own dignity, value, or self-esteem.

On the other hand, Swift is a humorist of a dubious kind. I read *Gulliver's Travels* so long ago that I remember little of it, but I do remember that it is a satire against something—which does not project what the author is *for*. He satirizes all kinds of social weaknesses, but upholds nothing.

In a more modern style, Dorothy Parker laughs in a nasty, bitter way. She is regarded as a sensitive writer, yet manages to deal humorously with the most heartbreaking subjects possible, like lonely old maids or ugly, undesired women.

Humor as the exclusive ingredient of a story is a dubious form of writing. While some people have acquired great skill at it, such humor is philosophically empty because it is merely destruction in the name of nothing.

In sum, humor is a destructive element. If the humor of a literary work is aimed at the evil or the inconsequential—and if the positive is included—then the humor is benevolent and the work completely proper. If the humor is aimed at the positive, at values, the work might be skillful literarily, but it is to be denounced philosophically. This is true also of satire for the sake of satire. Even if the things satirized *are* bad and deserve to be destroyed, a work that includes no positive, but only the satirizing of negatives, is also improper philosophically.

Fantasy

Several different forms of literature can be classified as fantasy.

To begin with, there are stories laid in the future, as, for instance, *Atlas Shrugged* and *Anthem*, Orwell's *Nineteen Eighty-four*, and a whole string of older books. Strictly speaking, this type of fiction is not fantasy, but merely the projection of something in time. Its justification is to show the ultimate consequences of some existing trend, or some other application to actual reality. The only rule about it is that it should not be purposeless (which is so general a rule that it applies to all literature). To place something in the future merely for the sake of placing it in the future would be irrational.

Then there is science fiction, which projects future inventions. There are magic stories, which project supernatural powers (fairy tales would be an example). There are ghost and horror stories. And there are stories about the hereafter—about heaven and hell.

All of these forms are rational when they serve some abstract purpose applicable to reality.

Most of Jules Verne's science fiction presented extensions of the discoveries of his time; for instance, he wrote stories about dirigibles and submarines before these were actually invented. This was merely a literary exaggeration of an existing fact. Since inventions exist, it is legitimate for a writer to project new and greater ones.

The same principle applies to fairy tales. Stories like *The Magic Carpet* and *Cinderella* are justified even though the events are metaphysically impossible, because those events are used to project some idea which *is* rationally applicable to human beings. The author indulges in metaphysical exaggeration, but the *meaning* of the story is applicable to human life.

The best example of this kind of fantasy is *Dr. Jekyll and Mr. Hyde*. The literal subject of the story—a man who changes himself physically into a monster—is impossible, but this is only a symbolic device to convey a psychological truth. The story is a study of a man with contradictory premises. By drinking a special medicine, Dr. Jekyll indulges in the fun of turning himself into a monster. At first he is able to control the process, but then he reaches a stage where he cannot control it anymore, where he turns into the monster whether he wants to or not. This is what in fact happens to bad premises: at first they might be hidden or controlled, but if unchecked, they take control of a personality.

Dr. Jekyll and Mr. Hyde is a brilliant psychological study projected into a fantastic form. The issue of the story is rationally applicable to human life, and very important.

A similar example is *Frankenstein*, the story of a man who creates a monster that gets out of his control. The meaning of the story is valid: a man must bear the consequences of his actions and should be careful not to create monsters that destroy him. This is a profound message, which is why the name Frankenstein has become almost a generic word (like Babbitt).

There are some interesting stories which project heaven or hell—for instance, the play *Outward Bound*. The characters are passengers on a ship who discover that they are in fact all dead and are now going to the Last Judgment. They start as a superficial collection of people—and then the author projects them in sharp, essential relief as they learn that they are soon to meet an examiner who will decide what happens thereafter. It is not a profound play, but its purpose is human characterization. Again, this fantasy has an application to actual human reality.

The movie *Here Comes Mr. Jordan* [1941] was a fascinating psychological story about a deceased prizefighter whose soul comes back to earth. He is not supposed to be dead—there has been some mistake in heavenly bookkeeping—so he is sent back in the body of a millionaire who has just died. By assuming that millionaire's existence, he learns a different way of life. Since a rational human issue was involved, the story was very interesting.

What kinds of fantasies are not justified? Those with no intellectual or moral application to human life—for instance, the movies about man-sized ants from another planet invading the earth. "Wouldn't it be horrible if ants suddenly conquered the earth?" Well, what if they did? If those ants at least symbolized some special evil—if, like animals in a fable, they represented dictators or humanitarians or other human monsters—such a story would be valid. But fantasy for the sake of fantasy is neither valid nor interesting.

In H. G. Wells's *The War of the Worlds*, men cannot defeat the

Martian invaders, but the germs of the common cold can. Like the rest of Wells's novels, this one appears to have profound meaning, but it actually does not. That the Martians are killed by cold germs is a nasty satirical touch, suitable at most for a clever short story. All it says is that nature can do what man cannot—and you do not write a whole novel merely to illustrate that one point. Wells tucks his message in at the end to give an allegedly redeeming meaning to what is only fantasy for fantasy's sake.

I know of no ghost or horror stories that I would classify as valid.

In *The Song of Bernadette*, the author presents the story of Bernadette of Lourdes [including her divine visions] as if it were fact. The story has no validity for anyone except those who choose to believe it, but it is not a fantasy. It is a religious tract.

One could make the point that all religion is a fantasy. Religion is not, however, fantasy for fantasy's sake. It has a much more vicious motive: the destruction of human life and the human mind. Religion uses fantastic means to prescribe a code of morality; therefore, it claims a relationship to human life. This raises the issue: Should man be guided by mystical dogma? But speaking in literary, not philosophical, terms, religious stories are distortions of reality for a purpose applicable to human life—although one would certainly be justified in fighting the purpose.

Pulp-magazine thrillers, which often have good plots, are devoid of any value application to reality. An example is a little pocketbook Leonard Peikoff once gave me. I had asked him if he knew of a good plot story, because I am miserably bored by any other kind, and he gave me one called *Seven Footprints to Satan*. It is the story of a man who becomes the prisoner of an archvillain who pretends that he is Satan and creates horrible evils for the sole purpose of stealing jewelry from museums and amusing himself by playing chess with human beings. The story is exciting in the sense that the writer knows how to keep up his suspense and mystery and when to introduce the unexpected—but the total has no meaning whatever. It lacks even the meaning of a good detective story or Western, which presents, in primitive terms, the conflict of good and evil.

A detective story is applicable to human life since crimes and murders *are* committed, and it has a crude moral pattern: the good fights the evil and always wins. But in the above type of science fiction or fantasy thriller, the message is not that the good wins in human life, even though the hero might escape. The values involved are meaningless and inapplicable to this earth.

You have probably heard the Romantic school of writing called "escape literature." The pulp-magazine type of thriller *is* an escape, but not in the usual sense. It is not merely an escape from the drudgery of one's existence (which would be a legitimate form of enjoyment); it is an escape from values and from the mind. The only thing that can make a story exciting and hold a reader's interest is some value at stake. In a thriller of the above kind, which features a fantastic and impossible villain, the escape for the reader consists of *dropping* all concern with values. He has the advantage of reading about a struggle, yet he can learn from the story no abstraction applicable to himself.

This school of literature tells the reader that there *are* values, except that they do not apply to his life. "Yes, you can have thrilling purposes and adventures, but they have nothing to do with your life on earth." Strangely enough, this cheap pulp literature is the expression of a religious metaphysics and morality: values *do* exist somewhere—on Mars or in another dimension—but not on earth.

This school includes all fantasies and all science fiction or general adventure thrillers which present issues without any possible counterpart in reality—issues without any application, abstract or symbolic, to the reader's own life. It also includes the lesser costume dramas. The better ones do present some issue that applies to modern life (usually in a very generalized way); but the cheaper historical novels, which consist of nothing but duels and swinging from chandeliers, have no moral beyond the hero winning the girl or the buried gold.

Symbolism

Symbolism is the concretization of an idea in an object or person representing that idea.

An example of symbolic writing is morality plays. Just as fairy tales present the good fairy and the bad fairy, so morality plays present moral abstractions by means of human figures like an embodied Justice or an embodied Virtue. The figures do not represent *characteristics* [as in Romantic fiction]; they represent the abstractions themselves as a kind of Platonic archetype. This is a crude dramatic form, but legitimate if the symbolism is made clear.

Dr. Jekyll and Mr. Hyde is symbolic insofar as physical shapes represent a psychological conflict, Mr. Hyde being a symbol of psychological evil.

The one absolute in the use of symbolism is that a symbol should be legible; otherwise, the form is a contradiction in terms. This applies also to symbolism *within* works which are not symbolic as a whole. My use of the dollar sign in *Atlas Shrugged* is an example: I establish its meaning, and when I later refer to it, I do so on that basis. Similarly, when writers of religious stories use the cross, it is clear what that cross stands for. But when authors introduce all kinds of triangles or sawed-off pyramids, and nobody knows what it means, that is outside the bounds of rational propriety. Or take Kafka, or any such modernist; if nobody knows what the alleged symbol represents, one cannot even call it symbolism.

When, at the end of Part II of *Atlas Shrugged*, Dagny follows Galt into the sunrise, that is symbolism. It is even a trite symbol, but so appropriate that it was legitimate. Literally, she is following his plane late at night, and by the locale of the action he has to go east (which I carefully planned long in advance). Symbolically, she has been in the dark during all of the story, but now she is about to see the sunrise—and the first light comes from the wings of Galt's plane.

Using the sunrise, or any form of light, as a symbol of the good or the revelation is a bromide, but it is a bromide of the kind that love is: it is so wide and fundamental that you cannot avoid it. What will make *your* use of it a bromide or not is whether or not you bring any originality to the subject.

It is not a good method to introduce symbolic *sequences* into an otherwise realistic story. For instance, some books have dream sequences which are supposed to be symbolic, but which are always completely unclear. This is a bad mixture of methods. It cannot be justified because it destroys the reality of the story. (It is proper, however, in musicals. In musicals, anything goes, the only rule being imagination.)

Tragedy and the Projection of Negatives

The justification for presenting tragic endings in literature is to show, as in *We the Living*, that the human spirit can survive even the worst of circumstances—that the worst that the chance events of nature or the evil of other people can do will not defeat the proper human spirit. To quote from Galt's speech in *Atlas Shrugged*: "Suffering as such is not a value; only man's fight against suffering, is."

Here I speak of *philosophical* justification, not literary. As far as literary rules go, you can present anything you wish—you can write a story in which everybody is destroyed, the theme then being that man has no chance and destruction is his fate. There are many such stories, some of them well written. But to present suffering for the sake of suffering is totally wrong philosophically; and literarily it makes for a pointless story.

In *We the Living*, all the good people are defeated. The philosophical justification of the tragedy is the fact that the story denounces the collectivist state and shows, metaphysically, that man cannot be destroyed by it; he can be killed, but not changed or negated. The heroine dies radiantly endorsing life, feeling happiness in her last moment because she has known what life properly should be.

Another proper tragedy is *Cyrano de Bergerac*, where the hero dies frustrated both as a lover and in his career as a poet. But he maintains his values to the end. The justification for this tragedy is precisely that nothing broke the hero's spirit—yet the author put every kind of disaster in his way.

Victor Hugo, who usually has unhappy endings, always presents his characters' suffering somewhat in the way that I do in *We the Living*. Even if a particular character meets with disaster, the tragedy and pain are never complete; they are not, metaphysically, the final word on man. Hugo never projects the overwhelming horror of pain that one finds in Naturalistic novels—for instance, in the suicide scene in *Anna Karenina.* (Conversely, enjoyment and happiness never go unchallenged in Naturalistic novels.)

In general, the creation of *only* the negative is a flaw, both philosophically and literarily.

The best example is Dostoevsky, who was a moralist, but who was never able to project what he considered good. (He attempted it in several novels, without success.) However, in presenting the evils he denounced, he was a master.

This is a flaw in his novels. They are, in a way, incomplete works of fiction. I like them as a spectacle of human intelligence and perceptiveness at work—the spectacle of what Dostoevsky's mind is able to identify and present. But after one finishes, one has only the satisfaction of having *learned* something about human nature, not the artistic satisfaction of having lived through an experience which is an end in itself. Reading his novels is anything but an end in itself.

The purpose of Dostoevsky's novels is more didactic than artistic. The artistic means are superlative; his technique is magnificent. But since art is primarily a presentation of values, Dostoevsky fails because he can project his values only by means of negatives. We know what he is against, but not what he is for; he is not able to project it. (The reason is that he is much too intelligent a man, and too good an artist, to do what he wanted, namely, to project successfully a Christian ideal.)

An example from another field is Goya, the artist who is a master at presenting unspeakable horrors. You might be familiar with the horrible scenes he painted of the Napoleonic Wars in Spain. It is said—and is probably true biographically—that his purpose was to denounce the horror of war. But I would question Goya's motive, and Dostoevsky's. An artist, whether he identifies it or not, *is*, after all, busy projecting his values—and it requires a certain amount of *fascination with evil,* of holding evil as a value, to devote a whole work exclusively to that. Dostoevsky openly projected such fascination.

I read a novel for one purpose only, and to me no amount of literary skill is of equal importance.

I read a novel for the purpose of seeing the kind of people I would want to see in real life and living through the kind of experience I would want to live through. To those who say that this is a limited use of fiction, my answer is: No—because for any other purpose, nonfiction is better. If I want to learn something, I can learn it from nonfiction. But in the one realm where nonfiction cannot do as well—the realm of values and their concretization in human reality—nothing can take the place of art, and specifically of fiction.

Since that is the primary purpose of art, that is what I personally enjoy most and the only thing that counts.

I would not want to live through a story by Dostoevsky. I admire him very much, but only literarily; I do not enjoy reading his stories. I enjoy Victor Hugo. I do not share his ideas and do not always approve of his tragic endings; nevertheless, he is the writer nearest to creating the kind of people and events I would like to observe or live with.

That is my personal enjoyment of literature, and it is not subjective. By "personal," I only mean "mine"—and I can defend and prove my standard in every respect.

This course is part of the proof.

INDEX